Data Association for Multi-Object Visual Tracking

Synthesis Lectures on Computer Vision

Editors
Gérard Medioni, *University of Southern California*
Sven Dickinson, *University of Toronto*

Synthesis Lectures on Computer Vision is edited by Gérard Medioni of the University of Southern California and Sven Dickinson of the University of Toronto. The series publishes 50- to 150 page publications on topics pertaining to computer vision and pattern recognition. The scope will largely follow the purview of premier computer science conferences, such as ICCV, CVPR, and ECCV. Potential topics include, but not are limited to:

- Applications and Case Studies for Computer Vision
- Color, Illumination, and Texture
- Computational Photography and Video
- Early and Biologically-inspired Vision
- Face and Gesture Analysis
- Illumination and Reflectance Modeling
- Image-Based Modeling
- Image and Video Retrieval
- Medical Image Analysis
- Motion and Tracking
- Object Detection, Recognition, and Categorization
- Segmentation and Grouping
- Sensors
- Shape-from-X
- Stereo and Structure from Motion
- Shape Representation and Matching

- Statistical Methods and Learning

- Performance Evaluation

- Video Analysis and Event Recognition

Data Association for Multi-Object Visual Tracking
Margrit Betke and Zheng Wu
2016

Ellipse Fitting for Computer Vision: Implementation and Applications
Kenichi Kanatani, Yasuyuki Sugaya, and Yasushi Kanazawa
2016

Computational Methods for Integrating Vision and Language
Kobus Barnard
2016

Background Subtraction: Theory and Practice
Ahmed Elgammal
2014

Vision-Based Interaction
Matthew Turk and Gang Hua
2013

Camera Networks: The Acquisition and Analysis of Videos over Wide Areas
Amit K. Roy-Chowdhury and Bi Song
2012

Deformable Surface 3D Reconstruction from Monocular Images
Mathieu Salzmann and Pascal Fua
2010

Boosting-Based Face Detection and Adaptation
Cha Zhang and Zhengyou Zhang
2010

Image-Based Modeling of Plants and Trees
Sing Bing Kang and Long Quan
2009

Data Association for Multi-Object Visual Tracking

Margrit Betke and Zheng Wu

ISBN: 978-3-031-00688-3   paperback
ISBN: 978-3-031-01816-9   ebook

DOI 10.1007/978-3-031-01816-9

A Publication in the Springer series

SYNTHESIS LECTURES ON COMPUTER VISION

Lecture #9

Series Editors: Gérard Medioni, *University of Southern California*
                Sven Dickinson, *University of Toronto*

Series ISSN

Print 2153-1056   Electronic 2153-1064

Data Association for Multi-Object Visual Tracking

Margrit Betke
Boston University

Zheng Wu
The Mathworks, Inc.

SYNTHESIS LECTURES ON COMPUTER VISION #9

ABSTRACT

In the human quest for scientific knowledge, empirical evidence is collected by visual perception. Tracking with computer vision takes on the important role to reveal complex patterns of motion that exist in the world we live in. Multi-object tracking algorithms provide new information on how groups and individual group members move through three-dimensional space. They enable us to study in depth the relationships between individuals in moving groups. These may be interactions of pedestrians on a crowded sidewalk, living cells under a microscope, or bats emerging in large numbers from a cave. Being able to track pedestrians is important for urban planning; analysis of cell interactions supports research on biomaterial design; and the study of bat and bird flight can guide the engineering of aircraft. We were inspired by this multitude of applications to consider the crucial component needed to advance a single-object tracking system to a multi-object tracking system—data association.

Data association in the most general sense is the process of matching information about newly observed objects with information that was previously observed about them. This information may be about their identities, positions, or trajectories. Algorithms for data association search for matches that optimize certain match criteria and are subject to physical conditions. They can therefore be formulated as solving a "constrained optimization problem"—the problem of optimizing an objective function of some variables in the presence of constraints on these variables. As such, data association methods have a strong mathematical grounding and are valuable general tools for computer vision researchers.

This book serves as a tutorial on data association methods, intended for both students and experts in computer vision. We describe the basic research problems, review the current state of the art, and present some recently developed approaches. The book covers multi-object tracking in two and three dimensions. We consider two imaging scenarios involving either single cameras or multiple cameras with overlapping fields of view, and requiring across-time and across-view data association methods. In addition to methods that match new measurements to already established tracks, we describe methods that match trajectory segments, also called tracklets. The book presents a principled application of data association to solve two interesting tasks: first, analyzing the movements of groups of free-flying animals and second, reconstructing the movements of groups of pedestrians. We conclude by discussing exciting directions for future research.

KEYWORDS

multi-object tracking, multi-target tracking, data association, multi-view tracking, multi-camera tracking, tracklet association, tracklet linking, tracklet stitching, tracking evaluation, MOT evaluation, Bayesian recursive filter, Bayesian multi-target tracking, Bayesian multi-object tracking, people tracking, animal tracking, group tracking, tracking bats, tracking birds

Contents

Preface

This book is designed to give an overview and introduction to the exciting field of visual tracking. It focuses on data association, which is needed when multiple objects must be followed through time. The tracking problem becomes particularly challenging in dense situations when numerous objects of interest have to be tracked simultaneously. These could be twenty-two soccer players in a stadium, fifty bats in the sky, or a hundred cells in a petri dish.

Both authors have contributed original research to the field of multi-object tracking. The first author wrote her first research paper on multi-object tracking in 1996. She has since designed computer-vision systems for tracking cars, people, bats, birds, and cells. The second author, her former Ph.D. student, postdoc, and now esteemed colleague, wrote his dissertation on "Occlusion Reasoning for Multiple Object Visual Tracking" at Boston University in 2012. He is particularly known for his work on tracking flying animals with multiple cameras and coupling multi-object detection and data association in one global optimization framework.

This book describes some of the authors' own work which was supported financially by the National Science Foundation (IIS-1421943, IIS-0910908, IIS-0855065, IIS-0326483, IIS-0308213, CNS 0202067), the Office of Naval Research (024-205-1927-5), and the Air Force Office of Scientific Research. The authors are thankful for these grants and stress that any opinions, findings, and conclusions or recommendations expressed in this book are those of the authors and do not necessarily reflect the views of these funding agencies.

The authors thank the current and former members of the Image and Video Computing Research Group at Boston University for sharing their insights. Dr. Matej Kristan and Dr. Michael Felsberg gave us valuable feedback to improve the presentation of this book. We are also grateful for our parents and family members for their continuous support, and dedicate this book to them.

Margrit Betke and Zheng Wu
Boston, Massachusetts
September 2016

CHAPTER 1

An Introduction to Data Association in Computer Vision

Research on multi-object tracking has a long history in computer vision. The first systems recorded image sequences with a single video camera. In recent years, imaging systems that use several cameras with overlapping fields of view have become attractive because they enable stereoscopic reconstruction of three-dimensional (3D) object trajectories. Analyzing 3D trajectories is particularly useful when the task is to track a large number of objects [Wu et al., 2009a]. In large groups, objects may not be visible in all camera views at all times because they occlude each other. Their 3D positions may then only be inferred from information about their paths before and after the occlusion event. It is therefore important that the multi-object tracking system has an "occlusion reasoning" component. At the center of this component lies "data association." Across-time data association is the process of matching currently observed objects with previously established object tracks. Across-view data association matches objects that appear in the views of different cameras. This book first focuses on across-time data association for single-camera systems and then discusses solutions that combine across-time and across-view strategies for multi-object tracking with multi-camera systems. The book provides a comprehensive description of traditional approaches, algorithmic developments, implemented systems, and application results.

1.1 CHALLENGES

Although the problem of multi-object tracking has been studied for decades, research toward robust solutions that specifically work with visual data is ongoing. There are various reasons why visual tracking is so difficult. Before an object can be tracked, it must be detected. Methods for object detection, however, still lack robustness. Another reason is the poor scalability of the traditional data association methods to handle large numbers of objects. Frequent inter-object occlusions are sources of difficulties for both object detection and data association methods. When occlusion happens, detection and data association often become unreliable because assumptions break that existing tracking systems make. Innovative systems are needed that can reason successfully about occlusion. "Occlusion reasoning" is a crucial component to boost the accuracy of a tracking system. Occlusion reasoning is therefore an important focus of this book.

Two directions of research may be followed to tackle the problem of occlusion. One is to develop batch processing solutions, which means, instead of making decisions based on the observations seen so far, one decision at a time (online), decisions are made based on the observations from the entire tracking sequence (offline, in a batch). The offline approach is only viable if the specific task to be solved does not require a real-time analysis but permits a wait for the solution until after the full video has been recorded. A compromise on the timing requirement yields an algorithm that computes results online but delayed, based on the observations in a sliding window of time.

The second research direction this book discusses is to provide multiple views of the objects with the expectation that, when occlusion happens in one view, it may not happen in other views that can be then used to track objects more reliably. This approach, however, introduces the need for across-view data association, a challenging process that requires spatial calibration of the cameras.

A third direction of research in multi-object visual tracking concerns the efficiency of algorithms. How fast a system computes and interprets object trajectories is a central question that is particularly important when large groups of individuals must be tracked. To speed up the tracking process, ongoing research in offline visual tracking considers a version of data association that matches trajectory segments, "tracklets," instead of position measurements.

1.2 RELATED TOPICS BEYOND THE SCOPE OF THIS BOOK

This book does not consider the tracking problem in a camera network, as, for example, the companion book by Roy-Chowdhury and Song [2011] in this series. Although camera networks may include cameras with overlapping fields of view, typically these networks have large numbers of cameras with distinct fields of views, so as to cover large areas for surveillance. This book also does not describe object detectors used in tracking and the various appearance-based tracking methods.

Multi-object tracking systems can be used for visual counting of people or animals in a crowded scene [Betke et al., 2008]. The denser the crowd is, the more difficult it becomes to count accurately. There are methods that estimate the size of a crowd without explicitly tracking each member of the crowd [Chan and Vasconcelos, 2012, Idrees et al., 2013, Lempitsky and Zisserman, 2010]. These methods do not use individual object detectors or trackers, and thus do not need data association of individuals. Describing these methods is therefore beyond the scope of this book.

1.3 APPLICATION DOMAINS

The application domain for multi-object tracking that has been most widely studied in computer vision is pedestrian tracking. Surveillance is the motivation of many works that analyze the movements of people in outdoor or indoor environments. In this book, the focus is on tracking methods that involve large groups of people. Various methods for trajectory-based abnormality detection in a crowd, for example, have been proposed [Ali and Shah, 2008, Andrade et al., 2006, Brostow and Cipolla, 2006, Wang et al., 2008]. Street scenes are also analyzed for tracking multiple vehicles simultaneously [Betke et al., 2000].

In ecology and conservation biology, tracking systems are applied to study animal abundance and behavior. Censusing populations of animals is imperative for quantifying their ecological and economic impact on terrestrial and aquatic ecosystems and facilitating conservation efforts [Betke et al., 2008]. The behavior of caged and wild animals is investigated in laboratories and the field, respectively, with single or multiple camera systems. This book gives an overview of multi-object tracking systems used in ecology research.

From the perspective of a computer vision researcher, an important criterion to characterize the different application domains is whether the tracking system can make the assumption that the movement is constrained by a plane [Khan and Shah, 2006]. This plane may be the ground pedestrians walk on, the surface of a lake that ducks swim on, or the thin layer of hydrogel that live cells move in. Works that use this "ground plane assumption" for biological applications include two-dimensional tracking of swimming ducks [Lukeman, 2014], dancing bees [Veeraraghavan et al., 2008], meandering fibroblast cells [House et al., 2009], and foraging mosquitofish [Herbert-Read et al., 2011] and golden shiners [Katz et al., 2011] in shallow fish tanks.

Various tracking systems have been developed for biological applications that reconstruct unconstrained three-dimensional movements of animals in flight. A ground-plane assumption is then not made. Works that describe systems for studying flying insects include three-dimensional tracking of fruit flies [Wu et al., 2011a] and midges [Attanasi et al., 2014b]. Natural flocks of birds and colonies of bats have been studied in field experiments, including Mexican Free-tailed Bats [Betke et al., 2008, Theriault et al., 2014], European starlings [Ballerini et al., 2008b], and chimney swifts [Evangelista et al., 2015, Theriault et al., 2014].

In cell biology and biomaterial engineering, the behavior of live cells moving under the microscope is analyzed with visual tracking systems [Bise et al., 2009, House et al., 2009, Li et al., 2007, 2008b, 2006, Maška et al., 2014, Rittscher, 2010]. In medicine, the movement of multiple surgical clips surrounding abdominal tumors is tracked in preparation for radiation treatment [Betke et al., 2006].

The need of forensics specialists to interpret crime scenes motivated an out-of-the ordinary application of multi-object tracking—Zarrabeitia et al. [2014] developed a technique to reconstruct the three-dimensional trajectories of blood droplets.

Computer graphics is an important application area for multi-object visual tracking systems. Data-driven graphics approaches aim to learn from real-world trajectories of individuals in large groups. Analysis of measured trajectories and behaviors are then used to statistically train models for simulation of group motion. For example, Lee et al. [2007] extracted two-dimensional trajectories of individuals in a human crowd from an aerial view and then learned an agent model based on the features of the extracted trajectories to simulate a virtual crowd. Li et al. [2015] proposed a data-driven approach to simulate insects at different scales in order to generate virtual insect swarming. Wang et al. [2015] introduced a quantitative metric to compare the results of their simulations with real-world trajectories of insect swarms.

1.4   SIMULATION TESTBEDS

Simulation testbeds are valuable tools that are sometimes underutilized. They can be helpful for two tasks: (1) planning the recording of video data and (2) validating algorithm performance.

For the first task, simulation testbeds are useful for scientists who aim to collect new multi-object data sets and develop tracking systems that interpret these data. To capture videos of group motion with multiple cameras successfully, practitioners should consider simulating the experiment before conducting it. This is particularly advisable in scenarios where the motion of individual group members cannot be influenced by the experimenter, for example, when filming free-flying birds or bats. A simulation can help scientists to choose appropriate camera equipment and carefully consider the placement of their cameras.

Theriault et al. [2014] provided source code for simulating multi-camera experiments.

Towne et al. [2012] also simulated the design of stereo vision system with overlapping fields of view that was aimed to analyze flight trajectories of bats.

For the second task, virtual worlds with simulated multi-object motion can be created that serve as ground-truth synthetic data for algorithm validation. For example, Wu et al. [2009a] created a simulation of a column of virtual bats flying in tight formations. The simulation enabled Wu et al. to test their data association algorithm on a range of difficulty levels, from sparse to highly dense groups.

Another example for synthetic experiments to evaluate the performance of a tracking system was provided by Zarrabeitia et al. [2014]. They conducted a synthetic experiment with 100 trajectories of spherical objects that simulated the movement of blood droplets. The performance of the proposed method and alternative algorithms was then evaluated on these trajectories.

1.5   EXPERIMENTAL BENCHMARKS

Among the various application domains for multi-object tracking, analyzing the movements of people is widely studied in computer vision. Various benchmarks have been created, most notably, the PETS 2009 benchmark [PETS] and the MOTChallenge [Leal-Taixé et al., 2015a,b]. Chapter 9 critically discusses the common use of the PETS 2009 benchmark.

To address the need for a benchmark with video data from beyond the visible spectrum, Wu et al. [2014] created the thermal infrared video benchmark TIV that includes videos consisting of almost 64,000 frames of pedestrians, marathon runners, bicycles, vehicles, and flying animals. TIV comes with ground truth annotations and source code of baseline methods, which researchers can use to compare against.

A benchmark for comparison of cell-tracking algorithms was introduced by Maška et al. [2014] and tested by six algorithms submitted to the Cell Tracking Challenge workshop at the

IEEE International Symposium on Biomedical Imaging 2013. A winner of the challenge was not declared, and continuing research on multi-cell tracking relies on the use of the benchmark.

1.6   ORGANIZATION OF THE BOOK

This book is both an introduction to traditional data association methods and a comprehensive and critical compilation of state-of-the-art approaches. Consistency of notation across book chapters was sometimes sacrificed for the sake of consistency with the notation used in the original works. The reason for this notation choice was to make it easier for readers to learn about a method and its relationship to other works in this book and then deepen their understanding of the method by studying the original paper where it was introduced.

The remainder of the book is organized as follows.

Chapter 2 formally introduces the problem of data association and discusses traditional sequential data association methods. These include Joint Probabilistic Data Association (JPDA), Multiple Hypothesis Tracking (MHT), and the Global Nearest Neighbor Standard Filter (GNNSF), and they process video data when it arrives, frame by frame or in a "sliding window." After 30 years, these methods are still being used and improved over time, specifically to address the multi-object tracking problem.

Chapter 3 expands the introduction of classic methods to batch data association approaches. Batch approaches have access to the entire video data at once (i.e., do not have to wait until the data arrives sequentially), and therefore have the conceptual advantage that they can interpret the entirety of the visual information and thus potentially make fewer association mistakes. We will discuss the Markov Chain Monte Carlo Data Association (MCMCDA) method, the Network Flow Data Association (NFDA) method, and the Probabilistic Multiple Hypothesis Tracking (PMHT) method.

Chapter 4 introduces evaluation measures for tracking systems, in particular, the widely used *USC* and *CLEAR MOT* criteria. In addition to the classical measures of false positive and false negative track detections and precision in detection, these criteria also include track interruptions and switches. In this chapter it is argued that scores reported in the literature should be interpreted with a "grain of salt"—accepted but with a degree of skepticism about their utility. More research is needed on protocols for evaluating tracking systems.

Chapter 5 extends the problem of tracking multiple objects from a single camera to multiple cameras with overlapping fields of view. Here, in addition to *temporal* data association, i.e., frame-by-frame, the *spatial* data association, view-to-view, must be considered. The chapter discusses how to solve the two *across-view* and *across-time* data association steps for tracking dense groups of objects moving in free 3D space. Two methods, the "tracking-reconstruction method" and the "reconstruction-tracking method" are described that differ in the order in which the temporal and spatial associations are resolved.

Chapter 6 describes the track linking problem, which is also called the offline "tracklet stitch problem." The chapter describes a graph representation useful for track linking. The graph characterizes the object-interaction events that lead to occlusion in video sequences. A combinatorial algorithm is then introduced that processes this graph to resolve occlusion ambiguities. The chapter gives guidance on how to formulate the resolving process as a bipartite matching, minimum-cost flow, or set-cover problem, depending on the space-time characteristics of the occlusion events.

Chapter 7 presents three extensions of the traditional multi-object formulations. The first handles merged and split measurements, the second incorporates machine learning, and the third combines detection and data association into a single objective function.

Chapters 8 and 9 discuss the challenges that are particular to different application domains. The focus of Chapter 8 is the tracking of flying animals, which requires the reconstruction of three-dimensional trajectories. Chapter 9 reviews multi-object tracking systems for pedestrians and vehicles in urban scenes, which requires the reconstruction of planar motion.

Chapter 10 concludes with a discussion of future directions of research.

CHAPTER 2

Classic Sequential Data Association Approaches

The radar literature describes fundamental algorithms for tracking multiple targets within a dynamic system [Bar-Shalom and Fortmann, 1988]. This chapter reviews the most important sequential data association algorithms as they apply to the problem of visual tracking of multiple objects in an online process. Disambiguating measurement-to-track[1] associations for all objects in a scene may not be possible within one time step, especially if the objects have similar appearance. Nonetheless sequential tracking methods, in particular, the Global Nearest Neighbor Standard Filter (GNNSF) (Sec. 2.3) and the Joint Probabilistic Data Association (JPDA) method (Sec. 2.4) are popular, which must, in one time step, process the set of candidate assignments and decide on the most likely measurement-to-track associations.

If the requirement for sequential, time-step-by-time-step decisions can be relaxed, the likelihood of candidate associations can typically be estimated more accurately using a "look-ahead" or "deferred-logic tracking," approach. Uncertainties in the current time step may be resolved when evidence for or against a hypothesized association has been collected in subsequent frames. The classic deferred-logic method is Multiple Hypotheses Tracking (MHT) (Sec. 2.5). Multiple Hypotheses Tracking enumerates all possible combinations of object associations through time by building a hypothesis tree, and selects the best path through the tree, i.e., the path with the highest likelihood, as its solution. In practice, MHT requires various heuristics to prune the hypothesis tree in order to avoid its exponential growth [Cox and Hingorani, 1996].

Throughout this chapter, we assume a method for tracking a single object is given. Common choices are the well-known Bayesian recursive estimation techniques such as Kalman filtering [Brown and Hwang, 1997] or particle filtering [Isard and Blake, 1998, Pérez et al., 2002]. We here briefly describe the Kalman filter as an example for a single-object tracker (Sec. 2.1) that is particularly suited for multi-object tracking—each object is simply tracked by a separate Kalman filter.

---

[1]We use "measurement," "observation," and "detection" interchangeably in this book.

2.1 ADVANTAGES OF KALMAN FILTERS FOR USE IN MULTI-OBJECT TRACKING

The Kalman filter solves the "kinematic state estimation problem," which refers to computing the prediction $\hat{x}(t)$ of the n-dimensional state $x(t)$ of an object in a tracking scenario. In computer vision, the object state typically means its projected 2D position in an image and respective apparent velocity, or its 3D position and 3D velocity in the scene. The state can also include other time-varying quantities, for example, a point in the wing flap cycle of a tracked bird. The state equation of the Kalman filter has a Markov form:

$$x(t + 1) = A(t)x(t) + w(t), \tag{2.1}$$

where $A(t)$ is an assumed known state transition matrix, and $w(t)$ is zero-mean, white, Gaussian process noise with assumed known covariance $Q(t)$. The process noise $w(t)$ models randomness due to the movement of the object, for example, its sudden acceleration. Measurement $z(t)$ is modeled as a linear combination of the system state variable $x(t)$:

$$z(t) = H(t)x(t) + v(t), \tag{2.2}$$

where $H(t)$ is a $m \times n$ measurement matrix and $v(t)$ is zero-mean, white, Gaussian measurement noise with covariance $R(t)$. For readers unfamiliar with the Kalman filter, we recommend signal processing books [Bar-Shalom et al., 2001, Kay, 1993, Stone et al., 1999] and online resources (http://www.cs.unc.edu/~welch/kalman/) for a more detailed introduction. There are also short introductions to Kalman filtering in computer vision text books [Forsyth and Ponce, 2003, Sonka et al., 2008].

The Kalman filter has a number of advantages for application to multi-object tracking [Blackman and Popoli, 1999]:

1. Matrix $E[(x - \hat{x})(x - \hat{x})^T]$, which is also called the *state covariance matrix P*, provides a convenient measure of estimation accuracy. The reason is that, for each component of the state vector x, the Kalman solution $\hat{x}$ minimizes the Bayesian Mean Squared Error

$$\text{BMSE}(\hat{x}_i) = Diag(E[\,(x - \hat{x})(x - \hat{x})^T\,], i), \tag{2.3}$$

   where $Diag(P, i)$ indicates the ith diagonal element of matrix P. As long as the object dynamics and the measurement noise are accurately modeled, the BMS error is minimized (we recommend the book by Kay [1993] for an insightful derivation of the optimality of the Kalman filter). The estimation accuracy is needed as input to some data association functions.

2. The Kalman filter has a closed-form solution to maintain the prediction $\hat{x}(t|t - 1)$ and correction $\hat{x}(t|t)$ of the state x, as well as the prediction $P(t|t - 1)$ and correction $P(t|t)$ of the state covariance matrix P.

3. The Kalman filter automatically adapts to changing detection histories and thus handles missed detections due to occlusion by other objects.

4. The residual vector

$$\tilde{z}(t) = z(t) - H(t)\,\hat{x}(t|t-1),\tag{2.4}$$

also called the *innovation vector*, is the difference between the actual and predicted measurements with covariance matrix

$$S(t) = H(t)\,P(t|t-1)\,H^T(t) + R(t).\tag{2.5}$$

By increasing the elements of this residual covariance matrix S, it is possible to model the expected error due to uncertain data association and thus, at least partially, compensate for the effects of misassociation in dense multi-object tracking scenarios.

2.2   GATING

A technique called "gating" is used by many data association methods to reduce computation. Gating defines a search region for a list of measurement-to-track candidates and eliminates unlikely measurement-to-track candidates that are located outside this region. The validation gate is usually set up around measurements using the residual covariance matrix $S(t)$. Association is allowed within a gate if the norm d^2 of the residual vector $\tilde{z}(t)$ is bounded by G, i.e.,

$$d^2(t) = \tilde{z}(t)^T\,S^{-1}(t)\,\tilde{z}(t) \,\leq\, G.\tag{2.6}$$

Since the m-dimensional Gaussian probablity density f for the residual $\tilde{z}$ is

$$f(\tilde{z}) = \frac{1}{2\pi^{m/2}\sqrt{det(S)}}\,\exp(-d^2/2),\tag{2.7}$$

the gate G is an iso-probability contour obtained when intersecting a Gaussian with a hyperplane. The shape of the validation gate is a hyper-ellipsoid, as illustrated in Fig. 2.1, middle. The norm d^2 is assumed to have a chi-squared distribution with degrees of freedom determined by the dimension m of measurements [Blackman and Popoli, 1999].

2.3   GLOBAL NEAREST NEIGHBOR STANDARD FILTER (GNNSF)

Probably the simplest but most widely used data association method is the Global Nearest Neighbor Standard Filter (GNNSF). It considers all possible measurement-to-track assignments within appropriate gating regions and generates the most likely assignment hypothesis by solving a 2D binary assignment problem. The assignment hypothesis is used to set irrevocable assignments

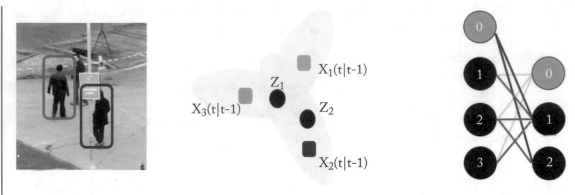

Figure 2.1: Example of data association problem with Global Nearest Neighbor Standard Filter (GNNSF). The scene contains three pedestrians walking toward each other. At time t, two measurements z_1 and z_2 were returned by the pedestrian detector, while one pedestrian who is occluded by the street sign was missed. Detections falling into the gating region of an object, shown as a shaded region, are potential assignment candidates. The gating region is typically a hyper-ellipsoid if the residual measurement vector $\tilde{z}$ is Gaussian distributed. For the GNNSF method, the cost of pairing of a measurement z and a predicted position $\hat{x}(t|t-1)$ is defined as the Mahalanobis distance between them. The cost to identify a missed detection or a false alarm also needs to be properly modeled with prior knowledge of detection and false alarm rates. GNNSF models the 2D assignment combinatorial problem as a bipartite graph where nodes on the left column represent the objects, and nodes on the right column represent the detections. Possible pairings are expressed as edges between nodes with their associated costs. The node with a zero index, also known as a "dummy node," is used as the placeholder for missing detections or false alarms. The optimal solution to this 2D bipartite assignment problem gives the best set of matchings such that, 1) every detection and object are assigned, and 2) the total cost is a minimum.

that cannot be modified by future data. A "toy example" to describe the GNNSF data association process is given in Fig. 2.1.

Briefly summarized, the GNNSF method consists of the following steps:

1. Predict the measurements and their covariances to estimate the validation gates.

2. Compute the cost for all possible measurement-to-track assignments within each gating region.

3. Formulate the 2D assignment problem and obtain a global optimal solution as the best assignment hypothesis.

4. Perform tracking by updating the state of each object and its covariance from the assignment result.

The first and last steps of the GNNSF method are standard procedures for Bayesian recursive filters such as the Kalman filter [Brown and Hwang, 1997] or the particle filter [Isard and Blake, 1998], and will therefore not be discussed here. The core step of the GNNSF method is the setup of the 2D assignment problem so that it can be solved efficiently. Formally, the objective function is

$$
\min_{x_{i,j}} \sum c_{i,j} x_{i,j}
$$
$$
s.t. \sum_{i:i>0} x_{i,j} = 1
$$
$$
\sum_{j:j>0} x_{i,j} = 1
$$
$$
x_{i,j} \in \{0, 1\} \tag{2.8}
$$

where $x_{i,j}$ is the binary variable to assign the ith object to the jth measurement, and $c_{i,j}$ is the corresponding cost. It is also common to add a "dummy object" and a "dummy measurement," both indexed by zero, to represent missing detections and false alarms, respectively. The constraints enforce the assignment solution to be exhaustive and exclusive, except for the dummy object/measurement.

In the optimization literature, the formulation in Eq. (2.8) is known as the bipartite matching problem [Bertsekas, 1991, Veenman et al., 2001]. Various polynomial-time algorithms solve the problem, such as the Hungarian method (also called the Munkres or Kuhn-Munkres method), the Auction method, and the Jonker-Volgenant-Castanon (JVC) method [Bar-Shalom and Li, 1995, Bertsekas and Castañón, 1992]. The algorithms all have worst time complexity of $O(n^3)$, where n is either the number N of objects or M of measurements. Their average performance differs in practice depending on the range of the cost values. Readers may refer to the book by Bertsekas [1991] for details on these algorithms.

The most compelling advantages of the GNNSF method are its simplicity and scalability. The 2D assignment problem has been well-studied in the optimization literature, and the computation can be performed very quickly in practice. A careful design of the association cost is necessary, because GNNSF makes "hard decisions" on the data association without accounting for the possibility that they might be erroneous. In fact, very often GNNSF only works well when objects are widely spaced, or are distinctive in appearance (in the latter case, the cost function evaluates appearance dissimilarity). In addition, the object detector has to maintain a high detection rate and a low false alarm rate. When a Bayesian recursive filter is used, one way to improve GNNSF performance is to increase the entries in the covariance matrix to capture the uncertainty of possible misassociation [Nahi, 1969, Singer and Stein, 1971]. Alternatively, one may consider the uncertainty in association conditions by allowing a track to be updated by a weighted combination of all the measurements in its gate. This essentially leads to the Joint Probabilistic Data Association (JPDA) method, as we will discuss in the next section.

2.4   JOINT PROBABILISTIC DATA ASSOCIATION (JPDA)

The Joint Probabilistic Data Association (JPDA) method [Bar-Shalom and Fortmann, 1988] is a sequential tracking method like GNNSF. Unlike GNNSF, which updates the track based on a single measurement from the best assignment solution, JPDA takes all the measurements within the gate into account. In JPDA, the state estimate of a track is in the form of a weighted sum of contributions given by all the feasible measurements, i.e., the expectation over all the association hypotheses.

The JPDA method relies on a few assumptions:

1. The number of established objects, N, at the given time step must be known. This implies that the classic JPDA method does not explicitly handle track birth and termination.

2. Each object has its own motion dynamic and measurement models, e.g., Eqs. (2.1) and (2.2). The past state estimates of the objects, under the Markovian assumption, are given by sufficient statistics, such as mean and covariance.

3. Each object produces at most one measurement, and each measurement either originates from a unique object or from background clutter.

We use the notation $X^{(t)} = \{x_1, x_2, ..., x_N\}$ to define the set of N object states at time t and $Z^{(t)} = \{z_1, z_2, ..., z_M\} \bigcup Z^{(t-1)}$ the set of M measurements at time t and all the previous measurements up to $t - 1$. The task of the JPDA algorithm is to evaluate the conditional probability of the joint assignment event:

$$\theta = \bigcap_{j=1}^{M} \theta_{j,i_j} \tag{2.9}$$

where θ_{j,i_j} is the event that the measurement z_j originates from the object in state x_{i_j}, where $0 \leq i_j \leq N$.

The JPDA method first generates two matrices. The validation matrix Ω is a binary $M \times (N + 1)$ rectangular matrix that represents all feasible measurement-to-track pairings as the result of gating. Matrix Ω is defined as

$$\Omega = [\omega_{j,i}] = \begin{pmatrix} 1 & \omega_{1,1} & \omega_{1,2} & \cdots & \omega_{1,N} \\ 1 & \omega_{2,1} & \omega_{2,2} & \cdots & \omega_{2,N} \\ \vdots & \vdots & \vdots & \cdots & \vdots \\ 1 & \omega_{M,1} & \omega_{M,2} & \cdots & \omega_{M,N} \end{pmatrix}, \tag{2.10}$$

where $\omega_{j,0}$ means the jth measurement originates from background clutter, and for all $i > 0$, $\omega_{j,i} = 1$ if the jth measurement originates from the i-th object.

The feasibility matrix $\hat{\Omega}(\theta) = [\hat{\omega}_{j,i}(\theta)]$ describes that the joint event θ can be generated from the validation matrix Ω in Eq. (2.10). It has the same size as the validation matrix Ω and is defined by

$$[\hat{\Omega}(\theta)]_{j,i} = \hat{\omega}_{j,i} = 1 \quad \text{if event } \theta_{j,i} \text{ occurs.} \tag{2.11}$$

Each row of $\hat{\Omega}(\theta)$ has only one nonzero entry and each column (except for the first column) has at most one nonzero entry. This ensures the third assumption described earlier is fulfilled: Each object produces at most one measurement, and each measurement either originates from a unique object or from background clutter.

The next step of the JPDA method is to compute the probability of the joint event θ conditioned on all measurements $Z^{(t)}$ [Bar-Shalom and Li, 1995]. For its computation, the probability P_D of object detection is first determined experimentally. Indicator variable τ_j for the j-th measurement being generated from a true object, and indicator variable δ_i for the i-th object being associated with some measurement are used. The total number ϕ of false alarms must also be described, either with parametric or non-parametric models.

For a parametric version of JPDA, the Poisson probability mass function is typically chosen to model the number of false alarms ϕ:

$$\mu_F(\phi) = e^{-\lambda V} \frac{(\lambda V)^\phi}{\phi!}, \tag{2.12}$$

where V is the volume of the surveillance space (in 2D, the region of the image frame under observation; in 3D, the full observation volume) and λ is the spatial density of false alarms (average number of false alarms in the surveillance space). Using Bayes' rule, the probability of a joint event θ conditioned on all measurements up to the current time, $Z^{(t)}$, is then

$$p(\theta \mid Z^{(t)}) \propto \prod_j \{\lambda^{-1} f_{i_j}(z_j)\}^{\tau_j} \prod_i (P_D)^{\delta_i} (1 - P_D)^{1-\delta_i} \tag{2.13}$$

where

$$f_{i_j}(z_j) = \mathcal{N}(z_j; \hat{z}_{i_j}(t|t-1), S_{i_j}(t)), \tag{2.14}$$

and $\hat{z}_{i_j}(t|t-1)$ is the predicted measurement of object i_j with associated innovation covariance $S_{i_j}(t)$.

For the nonparametric version, a constant can be chosen to model the number of false alarms

$$\mu_F(\phi) = constant, \tag{2.15}$$

which gives the joint association probability

$$p(\theta|Z^{(t)}) \propto \phi! \prod_j \{V f_{i_j}(z_j)\}^{\tau_j} \prod_i (P_D)^{\delta_i} (1 - P_D)^{1-\delta_i}. \tag{2.16}$$

Once the probability $p(\theta|Z^{(t)})$ of the joint association event θ has been estimated using Eq. (2.13) or Eq. (2.16), the JPDA method computes the marginal association probability

$p(\omega_{j,i}|Z^{(t)})$, the probability that the jth measurement belongs to the ith object. This is achieved by summing the probabilities for all joint events θ in which the marginal event of interest $\theta_{j,i}$ occurs:

$$p(\omega_{j,i}|Z^{(t)}) = \sum_{\theta} p(\theta|Z^{(t)})\,\hat{\omega}_{j,i}(\theta). \tag{2.17}$$

These marginal probabilities then serve as the weights to update the state estimate $\hat{x}_i$ of each object:

$$\begin{aligned}
\hat{x}_i(t|t) &= E[x_i(t)|Z^{(t)}] \\
&= \sum_{j} p(\omega_{j,i}|Z^{(t)})\, E[x_i(t)|\,\omega_{j,i}, Z^{(t)}]
\end{aligned} \tag{2.18}$$

where the expectation of the state $x_i(t)$, given the event $\omega_{j,i}$ and all the measurements $Z^{(t)}$, can be computed following the regular state update procedure of the Kalman filter. Note that the summation in Eq. (2.18) implies that the states of the objects conditioned on the past measurements are mutually independent. For each object, JPDA updates the state of the object using all plausible measurements, each multiplied by the appropriate scalar weighting coefficient.

The computational burden of the JPDA algorithm is the generation of the feasibility matrix $\hat{\Omega}(\theta)$ and the evaluation of the marginal probability in Eq. (2.17). The number of feasibility matrices increases exponentially with the increase of number of measurements or objects, which prohibits many real-world applications with a large number of objects. Early attempts to speed up JPDA either completely circumvented the step to generate the feasibility matrices or improved the evaluation step using a tree structure [Fisher and Casasent, 1989, Roecker and Phillis, 1993, Van Wyk et al., 2004, Zhou and Bose, 1993]. Alternatively, recent work by Rezatofighi et al. [2015] tried to approximate the marginal probability with the m highest probability hypotheses. Such an approximation is based on the observation that, in practice, the m highest probability hypotheses account for almost all but a tiny fraction of the total probability mass.

We here briefly outline the approximation algorithm by Rezatofighi et al. [2015]. Instead of considering the full event space Θ of all possible joint events θ, the appoximation algorithm constructs a subspace Θ^m that only contains the most likely m entries in Θ based on their probability mass. The key is to select m so that $m \ll |\Theta|$. The summation in Eq. (2.17) is then reduced to m terms without scarifying too much accuracy. To find the m-best hypotheses, the method reformulates the data association problem as a 2D assignment problem, like the one in GNNSF, Eq. (2.8). The cost of pairing is modeled by the negative logarithm of the individual association probabilities. The objective function to find the best assignment can be expressed concisely as:

$$\min_{y\in\{0,1\}^n} C^T y, \quad s.t. \ \ Ay \le b, \tag{2.19}$$

where y is a binary indicator vector of length $N(M+1)$ such that element $y_n = \hat{\omega}_{j,i}$, and C is the cost vector with $c_n = -\log(p(z_j|x_i, \hat{\omega}_{j,i}))$. Matrix A and vector b are set to enforce the assignment constraints.

Let C_m be the m-th smallest objective value in Eq. (2.19), and $y^{(m)}$ be its corresponding solution. The solution $y^{(m)}$ can be obtained by successively adding a new constraint to the original problem:

$$
\begin{aligned}
y^{(m)} \quad &= \quad \underset{y}{\arg\min} \, C^T y \\
s.t. \quad & \quad Ay \leq b \\
& \quad y \neq y^{(l)}, \forall \, 1 \leq l < m.
\end{aligned} \tag{2.20}
$$

Instead of solving the above integer linear programming problem m times, a more efficient binary tree partition method was proposed to remove redundant constraints and inactive variables. Details of this algorithm were provided by Rezatofighi et al. [2015].

While the computational burden of the JPDA method can be reduced by various approximation approaches, other disadvantages of the method remain. First, track birth and termination are not explicitly considered in the formulation, so they have to be handled separately. Second, using all measurements to update the covariance matrix may exacerbate the risk of misassociation, because an increased covariance matrix may introduce additional measurement candidates in the gating region of a track. Finally, the JPDA method also suffers from a coalescence problem [Fitzgerald, 1985] where objects that are close to each other will tend to come closer because of the weighted state updates. To enhance the JPDA method, many extensions have been developed [Habtemariam et al., 2013, Kennedy, 2008, Lennart et al., 2011, Mahalanabis et al., 1990, Roecker, 1995], with applications on visual tracking of pedestrian and cells [Nezamoddini-Kachouie and Fieguth, 2007, Rezatofighi et al., 2012, 2015].

2.5   MULTIPLE HYPOTHESES TRACKING (MHT)

Multiple hypotheses tracking (MHT) [Reid, 1979a] is a deferred logic approach that hypothesizes all possible data associations over time and uses measurements that are received later in time to resolve ambiguities in the current frame. In contrast to the JPDA method, which decides on the most likely measurement-to-track associations at each time step, MHT propagates the current hypotheses in anticipation of subsequent data for better estimation. It also provides a principled formulation to handle the complete life cycle of tracks including birth, growth, and termination.

Although the computational cost for the exponentially growing number of hypotheses theoretically limits the scalability of MHT, many heuristic techniques have been adopted to enable a real-time performance. Although a successful implementation of the MHT algorithm is challenging, it is probably still the most widely used algorithm in the tracking community even after 40 years since its publication in the radar literature [Reid, 1979a] and 20 years since its publication in the computer vision literature [Cox and Hingorani, 1996]. MHT still provides competitive results computer vision datasets [Chenouard et al., 2009, Kim et al., 2015].

The key computation of MHT is to evaluate the probability of a new set $\Theta_l^{(t)}$ of assignment hypotheses at time t using Bayes' rule. This set $\Theta_l^{(t)}$ refers to the lth hypothesis of a joint cumulative event (set of association histories) at t and is made up of the parent event $\Theta_{m(l)}^{(t-1)}$ through $t-1$ and the offspring event (current association event) $\theta(t)$. The conditional probability of the set of association hypotheses $\Theta_l^{(t)}$ is:

$$
\begin{aligned}
P(\Theta_l^{(t)}|Z^{(t)}) &= P(\Theta_{m(l)}^{(t-1)}, \theta(t)|Z^{(t)}) \\
&\propto P(Z(t)|\Theta_{m(l)}^{(t-1)}, \theta(t), Z^{(t-1)}) \times P(\theta(t)|\Theta_{m(l)}^{(t-1)}, Z^{(t)}) \\
&\quad \times P(\Theta_{m(l)}^{(t-1)}|Z^{(t-1)})
\end{aligned}
\tag{2.21}
$$

where the first term on the right-hand side is the likelihood of the measurements $Z(t)$ at current time t given the association hypothesis, the second term is the probability of a current association hypothesis given the parent set $\Theta_{m(l)}^{(t-1)}$, and the last term is the prior term from the past time step.

We use N_d as the number of measurements associated with the previously $N_{m(l)}$ known objects, N_f as the number of false alarms, and N_a as the number of measurements associated with objects of new arrival. We further assume the number of previously known objects that are detected follows a binomial distribution with detection rate P_D, and both the number of false alarms and new objects follow the Poisson distribution with the density λ_f and λ_n, respectively. Following the derivations by Reid [1979b], one can show that the probability of the ith set of assignment hypotheses at time t is

$$
\begin{aligned}
P(\Theta_l^{(t)}|Z^{(t)}) &\propto P_D^{N_d} (1-P_D)^{(N_{m(l)}-N_d)} \lambda_f^{N_f} \lambda_n^{N_a} \left[\prod_{j=1}^{N_d} \mathcal{N}(z_j; \hat{z}_l(t|t-1), S_l(t)) \right] \\
&\quad \times P(\Theta_{m(l)}^{(t-1)}|Z^{(t-1)}).
\end{aligned}
\tag{2.22}
$$

The probability above is estimated iteratively within the hypotheses generation process. At each time step, when a new set of measurements is received, the set of hypotheses $\Theta_{m(l)}^{(t-1)}$ from the previous time step is carried over, and each of these hypotheses contains compatible tracks that do not share measurements. Then the hypothesis is expanded by enumerating all possible measurement-to-track pairings with the associated probability according to Eq. (2.22).

To reduce computational complexity, one should always try to perform clustering first, that is, grouping of objects without common measurements and handling each group separately. Another valuable heuristic is hypotheses pruning, which is based on the observation that many inconsequential, low-probability hypotheses do not need to be generated. The "m-best implementation" of MHT [Cox and Hingorani, 1996] prunes hypotheses so that only the m best hypotheses formed on the current measurements remain using Murty's method [Murty, 1968] for finding the m-best solutions to the assignment problem.

Both Reid's original implementation and Cox and Hingorani's m-best algorithm are called "hypothesis-oriented MHT." In the "track-oriented" version of MHT [Bar-Shalom and Li, 1995], hypotheses are recomputed using the newly updated tracks, and hypotheses formed on the previous time step are pruned. A special data structure called *track trees* is often adopted here to represent the hypotheses, as shown in Fig. 2.2. One argument to favor track-oriented MHT is that the number of tracks is typically smaller than the number of hypotheses, and so with track-oriented MHT, it is easier to achieve a real-time performance than with "hypothesis-oriented MHT" when computing resources are similarly limited [Blackman et al., 2001]. A comparison between the two versions of MHT implementations was provided by Blackman [2004]. Another interesting combinatorial formulation to MHT was independently discovered by Poore [1994] and Deb et al. [1997], where the most likely hypothesis (or the m-best hypotheses) can be found by solving a multi-dimensional assignment problem. We will explain this approach with more details in Chapter 6.

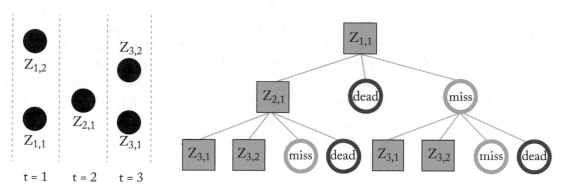

Figure 2.2: The data structure *track tree* for "track-oriented multiple hypotheses tracking." Left: An example with measurements in three consecutive frames, where $z_{t,i}$ represents the ith measurement at time t. Right: A track tree whose root is the first measurement $z_{1,1}$ in the first frame. Squares represent actual measurements. Green circles represent missed detections. Red circles represent track terminations. A second track tree is generated for the first frame, which has the same structure and labels except that its root is labeled $z_{1,2}$.

2.6   DISCUSSION

The three methods discussed in this chapter are representative sequential data association algorithms in three major categories. The Global Nearest Neighbor Standard Filter (GNNSF) is a heuristic approach that is prone to produce misassociations that are not recoverable. The Joint Probabilistic Data Association (JPDA) is a suboptimal method that uses Bayesian estimation of the object state by combining the information from all measurements that are possibly associated. Due to the underlying intractable enumeration of all joint association events, various approximation solutions have to be implemented in practice. The Multiple Hypothesis Tracking (MHT) is generally posed as the problem of maximizing the *aposteriori* probability of measurement-to-track associations given all measurements collected so far. It also has the problem of high computational complexity and various approximation implementations exist.

The data association problem is generally an NP-hard problem [Poore, 1994], especially when high-order constraints are encoded into the association, such as matching across more than two frames. No matter if an optimal method requires pure enumeration as for MHT [Reid, 1979a], or uses a multi-dimensional assignment formulation [Deb et al., 1997, Poore, 1994], a weighted maximum matching on a hypergraph [Shafique et al., 2008], or a maximum multi-clique formulation [Dehghan et al., 2015], we do not expect it to be efficiently computable for large problem sizes, unless $P = NP$. Therefore, the main goal to improve these classic methods is to develop techniques that efficiently approximate the computation without scarifying too much accuracy.

Finally, instead of using a separate filter for each object, modeling the multi-object tracking problem directly as a multi-object recursive Bayesian filtering problem is possible, where the collection of multi-object states is described as a set-valued state [Mahler, 2003]. Such a Bayesian filter, known as a Probability Hypothesis Density (PHD) filter, requires the use of advanced finite set statistics and avoids having to solve the data association problem explicitly. The interested reader is referred to the works by Mahler [2003] and Vo et al. [2008] for further information.

CHAPTER 3

Classic Batch Data Association Approaches

The sequential data association approaches discussed in the previous chapter are used for online processing of video data. The algorithms are executed whenever new data arrives, no matter if they are implemented to solve the association frame by frame or with deferred logic. In contrast, if the entire video can be considered for a tracking task, data association can be operated in batch mode. This has the advantage that association ambiguities are resolved using all the information available. In this chapter, we discuss classic approaches in this category, in particular, the Markov Chain Monte Carlo Data Association (MCMCDA) method (Sec. 3.1), the Network Flow Data Association (NFDA) method (Sec. 3.2), and the Probabilistic Multiple Hypothesis Tracking (PMHT) method (Sec. 3.3).

3.1 MARKOV CHAIN MONTE CARLO DATA ASSOCIATION (MCMCDA)

To handle a large number of objects in a dense environment with low detection probabilities and high false alarm rates, Oh et al. [2009] proposed a novel data association method based on Markov Chain Monte Carlo (MCMCDA) sampling. They showed that the single-frame version of MCMCDA is a *fully polynomial-time randomized approximation scheme* [Vazarani, 2003] for JPDA, which means that, for a given parameter $\epsilon > 0$, it produces a solution that is within a factor of $1 + \epsilon$ of being optimal while being polynomial in the size of the problem (number of tracks or measurements) and in $1/\epsilon$. Oh et al. [2009] also show that the multi-frame version of MCMCDA converges to the solution of the full Bayesian optimal filter. The method outperforms the traditional JPDA and MHT methods in difficult tracking conditions while still permitting real-time processing. In this section, we briefly introduce the multi-frame version. Details of the fundamental theory of MCMC sampling can be found in Bishop [2007].

The data association problem here is treated as a data partition problem, where a partition hypothesis $\omega \in \Omega$ is to separate the whole set of measurements $Z = \{Z_1, ..., Z_t, ..., Z_T\}$, where Z_t is the set of measurements for frame t, and T is the number of frames, into disjoint tracks $\{\tau_1, ..., \tau_k, ..., \tau_K\}$ and false alarms τ_0, where K is the number of tracks. As we discussed for tracking scenarios in which JPDA or MHT can be used, the *partition hypothesis*, also called *joint association event* should have the following formal properties:

1. $\bigcup_{k=0}^{K} \tau_k = Z$ and $\tau_i \cap \tau_j = \emptyset$ for every $i \neq j$,

2. $\|\tau_k \cap Z_t\| \leq 1$ for $k = 1, ..., K$ and $t = 1, ..., T$,

3. $\|\tau_k\| \geq 2$ for $k = 1, ..., K$,

where $\|\tau_k\|$ is the cardinality of the track τ_k. Note that the actual track τ_k is a sequence of the estimated states, but here, for simplicity of exposition, we assume it consists of its associated measurements. An example of a data partition hypothesis is illustrated in Fig. 3.1.

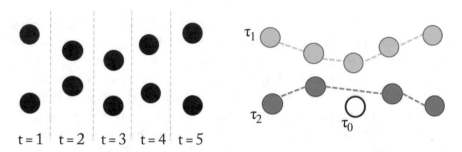

$$t = 1 \quad t = 2 \quad t = 3 \quad t = 4 \quad t = 5$$

Figure 3.1: Example of a data partition hypothesis. Left: The scene contains two objects moving in five frames. At each time step, two measurements are generated. Right: One hypothesis is to have two disjoint tracks τ_1 and τ_2, and assign one of the measurements in the third frame to the false alarm set τ_0.

To define the posterior probability of a partition hypothesis ω, given Z, the measurements in the entire video, we first denote a_t to be the number of new objects, c_t the number of objects from the previous time step that are continued to be seen at t, d_t the number of actual objects that are detected at time t, e_t the number of objects that exited (i.e., visible at $t - 1$, gone at t), and f_t be the number of false alarms. Similar to Eq. (2.21), the posterior probability of the partition hypothesis ω can then be computed as:

$$P(\omega|Z) \quad \propto \quad P(Z|\omega) \prod_{t=1}^{T} P_e^{e_t} (1 - P_e)^{c_t} P_d^{d_t} (1 - P_d)^{g_t} \lambda_n^{a_t} \lambda_f^{f_t}, \tag{3.1}$$

where $P(Z|\omega)$, P_e, P_d, λ_f, and λ_n are measurement likelihood, track termination probability, detection probability, and density parameters of the Poisson distribution for the number of false alarms and new objects, respectively.

The MCMCDA method [Oh et al., 2009] uses the Metropolis-Hastings algorithm [Robert and Casella, 2004], which is a Markov chain Monte Carlo (MCMC) sampler, to draw samples from the partition hypothesis space Ω such that the stationary distribution is the true posterior $P(\omega|Z)$ given in Eq. (3.1). At each state $\omega \in \Omega$, the algorithm proposes a new hypothesis $\omega' \in \Omega$

with the proposal distribution $q(\omega, \omega')$, and accepts this hypothesis with an acceptance probability $A(\omega, \omega')$ such that

$$A(\omega, \omega') = \min\{1, \frac{P(\omega'|Z)\, q(\omega', \omega)}{P(\omega|Z)\, q(\omega, \omega')}\}. \tag{3.2}$$

Otherwise, the sampler keeps the current hypothesis ω. Oh et al. [2009] designed eight types of proposal moves:

1. Birth move. The proposal randomly forms a new track using the measurements that are not assigned to any existing tracks.

2. Death move. The proposal randomly deletes one of the existing tracks.

3. Split move. The proposal randomly selects one of the existing tracks and splits it into two shorter tracks.

4. Merge move. The proposal randomly picks a pair of existing tracks that do not overlap in time and merges them into a single longer track.

5. Extension move. The proposal randomly selects one of the existing tracks and appends new measurements to it from the false alarm set.

6. Reduction move. The proposal randomly selects one of the existing tracks and removes part of the track and places it into the false alarm set.

7. Track update move. The proposal randomly selects one of the existing tracks and reassigns measurements to it.

8. Track switch move. The proposal randomly selects a pair of existing tracks and swaps the parts of the tracks that overlap in time.

A graphical illustration of the eight moves is shown in Fig. 3.2. Readers can refer to the paper by Oh et al. [2009] for details of the construction of the proposal distribution $q(\omega, \omega')$ for each type of move.

The MCMC sampling approach has been applied to several computer vision tracking problems [Benfold and Reid, 2011, Ge and Collins, 2008, Khan et al., 2006, Smith et al., 2005a, Yu et al., 2007], but it is currently not widely recognized in the community. One reason might be that randomized algorithms, compared to deterministic algorithms, yield experimental results that are considered to be more difficult to interpret. A more fundamental issue is that the convergence rate of the MCMC sampler still requires more research efforts [Lin and Fisher, 2012]. It has been shown that the MCMC chain in the multi-object tracking context has properties that theoretically guarantee convergence to the desired stationary distribution, given unlimited resources. Fortunately, the MCMC framework is flexible and allows specific domain knowledge to be incorporated in order to speed up convergence.

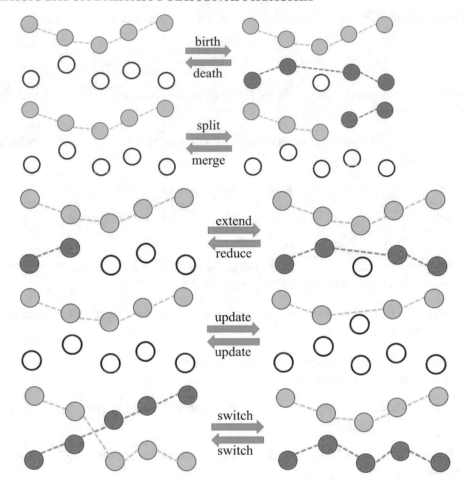

Figure 3.2: Example of MCMCDA moves. The MCMC sampler randomly chooses one of the eight moves at each iteration. Solid squares/circles are measurements assigned to tracks, rings are false alarms and dotted lines represent the association across time.

3.2   NETWORK FLOW DATA ASSOCIATION (NFDA)

The offline tracking framework known as the *network flow data association* (NFDA) method has gained popularity in the computer vision community over the past few years (e.g., [Wu et al., 2011b, Zhang et al., 2008]). The data association problem is typically casted as a minimization problem using a network representation and a computationally tractable objective function. The method takes all measurements into account, so it presumably achieves better accuracy than the online Global Nearest Neighbor Standard Filter (Sec. 2.3). The NFDA method is not a full Bayesian data association method because it only looks for an optimal solution among a set of single track hypotheses by estimating the maximum *a posteriori* probability (MAP) of this set, given the set of all observations. The set of possible hypotheses can be pruned by exploiting the fact that one object can only move along one trajectory. Unlike JPDA, MHT, and MCMCDA, which address an NP-hard problem, the network flow formulation permits the design of efficient algorithms that obtain a global optimal solution in polynomial time.

The classical network-flow data association method, first described by Castañón [1990], constructs a network in which every measurement returned from the detector in every frame is represented as a node in the network and every potential match between detections across time as an arc with an associated cost. We here use the terminology "network with nodes and arcs" and "graph with vertices and edges" interchangeably. We show an example of a tracking scenario represented by a cost-flow network in Fig. 3.3. The vertices of the cost-flow network represent the collected measurements at each time frame stacked in columns. The cost-flow network does

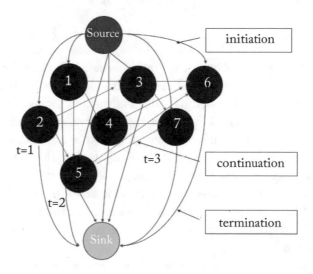

Figure 3.3: Data association as a minimum-cost network flow problem. A flow of amount 1 along a path from the source node (track initiation) to the sink node (track termination) represents the trajectory of a single object. Here, the measurements (1,2), (3,4,5), and (6,7) were made at time $t = 1$, 2, and 3, respectively, and are stacked into three columns. To ensure only mutually disjoint paths are allowed to flow through the measurement nodes, one can duplicate nodes and connect them with flow-capacity-one arcs (not shown here).

not have edges between the vertices in each column, it only has edges from column to column, and each edge represents a potential assignment of the measurements in two frames. A cost and a flow are associated with each edge in the graph. Each path (flow) through the graph represents an object trajectory. The representation includes two special vertices, "source" and "sink," to model track initiation and termination. The amount of flow from the source to the sink is equal to the number of object trajectories.

To ensure multiple tracks do not share the same detection, vertices in each time step are duplicated, and a single, unit-flow-capacity, zero-cost edge is added between them [Castañón, 1990]. By enforcing the upper bound on the flow of this edge to be 1, the paths (or flows) through the graph are guaranteed to be mutually exclusive. The goal is to push the right amount of flow into the network that corresponds to the trajectories of objects, i.e., sequences of associated measurements so that the total cost along the paths is minimum. This is a standard min-cost flow problem and can be defined as follows:

$$
\begin{aligned}
\min_{\mathbf{f}} \quad & \sum_i \sum_j c_{i,j} f_{i,j}, \\
\text{s. t.} \quad & \sum_i f_{i,n} = \sum_j f_{n,j}, \quad \forall\, n \in V, \\
& 0 \le f_{i,j} \le 1, \qquad \forall (i,j) \in E,
\end{aligned}
\tag{3.3}
$$

where $\mathbf{f}$ represents the paths through the graph (flows), V is the set of vertices, E is the set of edges, $c_{i,j}$ is the cost associated with each edge that links vertex i and j, $f_{i,j}$ is the flow variable associated with each edge, whose optimal value is always an integer for a cost-flow network.

The constraint set in Eq. (3.3) defines the conservation property that the amount of incoming flow is the same as the amount of outgoing flow at each node. The objective function in Eq. (3.3) is similar to the 2D assignment in Eq. (2.8). In fact, the 2D assignment in problem can be considered to be a special case of the min-cost flow problem.

As the number of objects present is unknown *a priori*, the NFDA method needs to search for the amount of flow that produces the minimum cost. However, one can link the sink node with the source node to form an equivalent "transportation problem" without explicitly specifying the amount of flow to be pushed.

It is important to notice that the network flow data association assumes that the cost function over a track is additive, i.e., it is a summation of edge cost along the path. Because of this (and unlike MHT or MCMCDA), it is not easy to extend the NFDA method to model measurement dependencies across more than two frames.

There are many efficient algorithms in optimization literature to solve Eq. (3.3), including the successive shortest path algorithm, the network simplex algorithm, the cost scaling algorithm, and a generic linear programming algorithm [Ahuja et al., 1993].

The network flow data association method was first proposed and solved by Castañón [1990], and then rediscovered by Jiang et al. [2007], Zhang et al. [2008]. Various extensions have been developed to enhance different aspects of the network model. Pirsiavash et al. [2011] proposed a greedy algorithm to embed non-maximum suppression inside the network optimization procedure, which achieved linear complexity so that it can process large input sequences and model long occlusions.

The network can be constructed on a predefined discretized grid, as opposed to the detection response, to force objects moving along the grid cells [Andriyenko and Schindler, 2010, Berclaz et al., 2009, Wu and Betke, 2016]. Since the path of the object does not need to pass through detection responses, missing detection and occlusion can be handled implicitly, at the expense of increasing number of nodes in the network. In order to speed up the process on a large network, Berclaz et al. [2011] proposed the k-shortest paths (KSP) algorithm by exploiting the special structure of the tracking problem. This algorithm is much more efficient than the general linear programming technique.

Andriyenko and Schindler [2010] enlarged the network to model the heading direction of an object by extending the functionality of the binary indicator variables to three consecutive frames. Multi-layer networks have also been designed to embed a long-range appearance model to associate detections across long time spans [Shitrit et al., 2011], or to support the tracking of objects of different categories [Wu and Betke, 2016]. Wang et al. [2014b] also enriched the network to encode different orientation of the object, and their network is able to track interacting objects of different categories.

Concluding our discussion of the NFDA method, we mention the work by Chari et al. [2015] who added pairwise costs between objects in the network to model mutual interactions in complex dynamic scenes with substantial clutter and partial occlusions. The objective function becomes quadratic in this work, and the data association problem becomes NP-hard again. A convex relaxation was designed to minimize pairwise costs using linear optimization, along with a principled "Frank-Wolfe style rounding procedure" to obtain integer solutions.

3.3   PROBABILISTIC MULTIPLE HYPOTHESIS TRACKING (PMHT)

Comparison of the aforementioned classic approaches shows that balancing the goals of accuracy and efficiency of data association is difficult. The GNNSF or standard Network Flow approaches provide efficient solutions by only considering the pairwise frame-to-frame associations using off-the-shelf optimization tools. The disadvantage of these approaches is that they do not capture measurement dependencies across more than two frames. In contrast, for Bayesian recursive filtering, i.e., the MHT or MCMCDA approaches, the association cost is the likelihood of generating measurements along the track given all the object states in history. This rich model, however, leads to an underlying NP-hard combinatorial optimization problem.

Computationally expensive data association methods have an enumerative nature due to the requirement of making "hard assignments" that explicitly map observations to tracks exclusively and completely. The novel idea of using "soft assignments," also known as Probabilistic Multiple Hypothesis Tracking (PMHT), was originally developed by Streit and Luginbuhl [1993]. They treated the assignments themselves as random variables or non-observed "missing data" and converted the data association problem into a "soft clustering problem" or "incomplete data estimation problem." The works by Gauvrit et al. [1997] on passive sonar and Yu et al. [2008] on pedestrian tracking are also along this direction.

Because PMHT requires neither enumeration of measurement-to-track hypotheses nor heuristics for approximation, it promises to be suitable for large-scale multi-object tracking problems. As we will see, the underlying optimization problem is not modeled by a discrete combinatorial but instead a continuous formulation that makes application of gradient-based optimization techniques possible.

The fundamental difference between PMHT and other classic approaches is that PMHT models the assignments for each measurement as independent random variables A. The goal is to evaluate the MAP estimate of all objects states $X = \{X(1), ..., X(T)\}$ given all observed measurements $Z = \{Z^{(1)}, ..., Z^{(T)}\}$, i.e.,

$$\hat{X} = \underset{X}{\text{argmax}} \ p(X|Z). \tag{3.4}$$

In this incomplete data estimation problem, the missing data are the assignment variables A and the complete data are the set $\{Z, A\}$. The assignment variable $A(t) = (a_1(t), ..., a_{m_t}(t))$ expresses an assignment hypothesis at time t for all m_t measurements. Component $a_j(t) = i$ indicates that object i generates measurement j at time t. For all $j = 1, ..., m_t$, the probability that measurement j originates from object i is $\pi_i(t) = p(a_j(t)=i)$. The constraint $\sum_{i=1}^{N} \pi_i(t) = 1$ for the assignment variables ensures that every measurement is generated from one object or from clutter. At each time step, $\Pi(t) = (\pi_1(t), ..., \pi_N(t))$ describes the respective probabilities for all N objects. With $\Pi = \{\Pi(1), ...\Pi(T)\}$, the parameters to be estimated by the PMHT method are the object states and assignment probabilities: $\{X, \Pi\}$.

PMHT uses the Expectation-Maximization (EM) algorithm [Dempster et al., 1977] to solve the multi-object tracking problem as a missing data estimation problem. The algorithm uses a weight parameter $w_{j,i}(t)$, which corresponds to the posterior probability that measurement j originates from the ith object given the current estimates for parameters X and Π. A flat start scheme can be used. The parameters at EM iteration $l + 1$ are updated as follows [Gauvrit et al., 1997]:

1. Update Π. $\forall t = 1, ..., T, \forall i = 1, ..., N$:

$$w_{j,i}^{(l+1)}(t) = \frac{\pi_i^{(l)} p(z_j(t)|x_i^{(l)}(t))}{p(z_j(t)|X^{(l)}(t), \Pi^{(l)}(t))} \tag{3.5}$$

$$\pi_i^{(l+1)}(t) = \frac{1}{m_t} \sum_{j=1}^{m_t} w_{j,i}^{(l+1)}(t) \tag{3.6}$$

2. Update X. Let X_i be the states $x_i(0), ..., x_i(T)$ of object i, $\forall i = 1, ..., N$:

$$X_i^{(l+1)} = \underset{X_i}{\arg \max} \{p(x_i(1)) \prod_{t=2}^{T} p(x_i(t)|x_i(t-1)) \prod_{j=1}^{m_t} p(z_j(t)|x_i(t))^{w_{j,i}^{(l+1)}(t)})\} \tag{3.7}$$

The EM iterations are repeated until some halting criterion is reached. The final estimated states X and assignments Π are retrieved from the last iteration. Note that the derivations above assume the number of objects are known ahead of time. In analogy to estimating the number of clusters in the clustering problem, the variational algorithm can be applied if we need to track time-varying number of objects.

The main issue with PMHT and its variants is that the inference algorithm typically used, EM or variational EM, has relatively slow convergence and is sensitive to the initial estimate of the model parameters. The algorithm can be trapped in a local minimum, which then yields a suboptimal solution. When a large number of objects needs to be tracked, many model parameters must be estimated. As a result, the problems of sensitivity to initial starting points and slow convergence present a challenge to applying these EM-type algorithms, and the scalability of the PMHT method therefore needs to be investigated more. Readers may refer to Crouse et al. [2009] and Springer [2012] for a more detailed analysis of PMHT.

3.4   DISCUSSION

The three methods discussed in this chapter are representative batch algorithms for data association that exemplify the challenge of solving the multi-object data association problem accurately and efficiently. Even when all the measurements are used to set up the batch processing problem, the optimal solution can be difficult to compute in practice. Both MCMCDA and PMHT rely on an iterative process to explore the hypothesis space, and they are typically able to converge to a reasonable solution after the first few iterations. But the risk of becoming trapped in a local minimum exists.

The properties of MCMCDA and PMHT regarding convergence have been derived directly from what is known about the convergence of the MCMC sampling and EM algorithms. It would be interesting to see if the problem of data association for multiple object tracking can provide additional problem structure to improve the theoretical analysis of convergence.

The network flow formulation is relatively easier to solve, but the model lacks flexibility to model high-order data dependencies. It does not provide a full posterior distribution either. Nevertheless, it currently seems to be more popular than the other two methods in the computer vision research community.

When the input sequence is very long, putting the entire sequence into a batch data association approach might not be practical due to limited computing resources. A sliding window technique is then typically adopted to process the entire sequence in several batches. There are overlapped frames between two consecutive batches, and the tracks obtained from the first batch can be used to initialize the second batch. For example, the determined associations from the first batch in the overlapped frames can be fixed in the second batch.

Finally, the classical sequential or batch data association approaches that we described in the last two chapters can be roughly classified into two categories:

1. Methods (JPDA, MHT, MCMCDA, PMHT) that compute a full distribution in the data association space from the prior knowledge, posterior beliefs, and the measurements, and

2. Methods (GNNSF, NFDA) that only compute a maximum likelihood or maximum-*a-posteriori* estimate from the possible set of data association solutions.

More modern data association methods in both categories will be discussed in Chapter 7.

CHAPTER 4

Evaluation Criteria

For quantitative evaluation of a multi-object tracking system, various measures have been proposed in the tracking performance literature [Bernardin and Stiefelhagen, 2008, Black et al., 2003, Kao et al., 2009, Kasturi et al., 2009, Ristic et al., 2011, Schuhmacher et al., 2008, Senior et al., 2001, Smith et al., 2005b, Theil et al., 2000, Wu, 2008].

Although it may be desirable to summarize the performance of a system by a single number, very often multiple measures reflect different aspects of a tracking system and therefore give a more complete profile. This book therefore follows the trend to use two sets of measures to evaluate the performance of a tracking system, namely the "USC measures" by Wu [2008] and the "CLEAR MOT" measures by Bernardin and Stiefelhagen [2008].

4.1 DEFINITIONS

We first describe a process for comparing the trajectories that are deemed to be the "ground truth," typically by visual inspection and manual annotation, and the trajectories computed by the multi-object tracking system. In this process, the inputs are a set of ground-truth tracks G and a set of system-generated tracks S. The output is a list of possible match pairs at each time step t. A pair (s, g) is deemed to be a potential match if its matching cost (or distance between s and g) passes a "hit/miss threshold" (we will discuss potential definitions of cost or distance and the threshold below).

Once a list of potential matches has been constructed, an assignment problem can be created to find the optimal one-to-one matches between system-generated and ground-truth tracks. Based on these matches, tracking errors, illustrated in Figure 4.1, which commonly occur in multi-object tracking, can be accounted for using the performance parameters described below.

The number of ground-truth tracks present in the current frame is denoted as g_t. The number of ground-truth tracks that are not matched, i.e., the number of misses (false negatives) is m_t. The number of system-generated tracks that are not matched (false positives) is $f p_t$. The number of system-generated tracks that are matched to different ground-truth tracks compared to the matches made at a previous time step is mme_t. This number is also called the number of mismatches or ID switches (see Figure 4.1). Given g_t, m_t, and mme_t for all the frames, the following CLEAR MOT measures can be computed:

- **Miss Rate (MR):** $\frac{\sum_t m_t}{\sum_t g_t}$,

- **False Positive Rate (FPR):** $\frac{\sum_t f p_t}{\sum_t g_t}$,

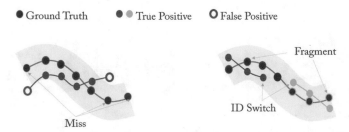

Figure 4.1: Accounting for common tracking errors of a multi-object tracking system. Left: A ground truth trajectory was not tracked for the first and the last two steps. Some predicted positions of the object by the system are outside the acceptable range defined by the hit/miss threshold (the shaded area), so they are classified as false positive matches. Right: A ground truth trajectory was not tracked at the fourth step, and re-matched to a different system-generated track later. A track fragment error and an ID switch error are counted in this case.

- **Mismatch Rate (MMR):** $\frac{\sum_t mme_t}{\sum_t g_t}$.

Since it is desirable to summarize the accuracy of a tracking system into a single number, the CLEAR MOT formulation includes a Multiple Object Tracking Accuracy (MOTA) score that takes into account false positives, missed targets, and identity mismatches:

- **Multiple Object Tracking Accuracy (MOTA):** 1–MR—FPR—MMR.

Finally, the precision of a tracking system needs to be measured. If the number of matched pairs in the solution is denoted as c_t and the distance (cost) between each matched pair i is denoted as $d_{t,i}$, then the precision is defined as:

- **Multiple Object Tracking Precision (MOTP):** $\frac{\sum_{t,i} d_{t,i}}{\sum_t c_t}$.

Additionally, it is useful to compute the following tracking quality scores, which we call "USC measures" since they were published in Bo Wu's doctoral dissertation at the University of Southern California [Wu, 2008]:

- **Mostly Tracked (MT):** the number of objects for which $\geq$ 80% of the trajectory is tracked, i.e., 80% of a ground-truth track has been matched to some non-empty set of system-generated tracks;

- **Mostly Lost (ML):** the number of objects for which $\leq$ 20% of their trajectories is tracked;

- **ID Switch (IDSW):** the number of identity switches $\sum_t mme_t$.

- **Track Fragments (FM):** the number of times ground-truth tracks are interrupted (untracked).

4.2   DISCUSSION

Among the criteria described above, MOTA is probably the most important number for ranking multi-object tracking algorithms, as it summarizes various possible tracking errors. If no errors exist, the MOTA score is 1. Because a system could generate an arbitrary number of false positive tracks, the MOTA score can become accordingly small. Its range is therefore $(-\infty, 1]$.

Note that even if two algorithms produce similar MOTA scores, they may present very different data association behaviors. One algorithm may produce lower track fragments as it excels at filling gaps in detection. The other algorithm may yield fewer ID switches as it builds a stronger discriminant model for the objects. Readers should always interpret these measures with a global view in order to better assess the quality of a MOT tracking system.

It is important for the reader to realize that the actual implementations of the measures can have variations, for example, existing implementations vary in the setup of the assignment problem occurred at each time step. Unfortunately, the research community has not converged on a single evaluation protocol for a given benchmark. We here list sources of inconsistencies and imperfections of the current evaluation criteria:

- The matching cost for a pair of tracks is application dependent and can be based on 2D or 3D information. In the 2D case, the cost is typically defined per frame as the "intersection over union," also called the Jaccard index $J(A, B) = |A \cap B|/|A \cup B|$ of the two bounding boxes A and B that are being compared. In the 3D case, the matching cost can be defined as the Euclidean distance between two 3D points that define the locations of the objects in 3D space.

- Once the cost definition is established, a "hit/miss threshold" on the cost is chosen that determines whether a particular matching is considered a candidate ("hit") or not ("miss"). A possible matching is considered only if the associated cost is above this threshold. In the 2D case, when the Jaccard index, which ranges between 0 and 1, is used, the commonly chosen hit/miss threshold is 0.5. Evaluation protocols that use different threshold values are sources of inconsistencies because they will result in different performance results.

- An evaluation protocol may choose to construct matching candidates independently at each time step, or give higher preference to the pairs that have been successfully matched in the previous frame. In the latter case, if a pair of tracks (g, s) is matched at step $t - 1$, and they are still in the potential matching list at step t, then (g, s) is matched at t regardless of its matching cost.

- The assignment problem can be solved with the Hungarian algorithm (Sec. 2.3) to achieve a global optimal solution, or with a greedy but faster algorithm to achieve a sub-optimal solution. Ideally, one would expect a single implementation to be a gold standard in order to perform a fair comparison among algorithms.

- Despite the common practice in the current research community of multi-object tracking to use the CLEAR MOT and USC measures, there are limitations in their utility. The measures are commonly adopted to evaluate the data association component of a tracking system while the detection component of the system has produced a fixed set of object detections. The scores are therefore dependent on this given set of detections. The measures do not reflect how a data association algorithm would respond to a set of inaccurate detections at different noise levels. It has been observed that the precision score MOTP becomes fairly flat once the quality of the input detections is fixed. The data association algorithm then has little impact on the precision score.

- While tuning system parameters to achieve high values for the described measures is legitimate, the sensitivity of the system to changes in parameter values is not reflected by the CLEAR MOT or USC measures. The *robustness* of a tracking system, i.e., its ability to effectively perform while its input data are altered, must be evaluated. An algorithm that is fine-tuned to certain data often poorly generalizes to other data, especially if the aim is to not have to change the parameters of the system significantly.

- An aggregated score like MOTA is difficult to interpret in practice and becomes problematic when sources of errors are weighed differently across applications (Fig. 4.2). For example, to facilitate comprehensive surveillance, an abandoned package must not be missed (i.e., no missed detections); and to count the number of people in a crowd, track identity switches do not affect the census. It would require a case-by-case study to adjust the relative importance of each error measure before aggregating them into a single score.

- Finally, popular performance measures like MOTA have been proven to lack the fundamental properties "monotonicity" and "error type differentiability" [Leichter and Krupka, 2013]. The "monotonicity" property means that the elimination of an error or the addition of a successful match should result in the measure to either improve or stay unchanged. The "error type differentiability" of a measure requires that it is informative about system performance with respect to each of the different basic error types. The fact that MOTA lacks both of these fundamental properties confirms that caution in using MOTA is advised. A multi-object tracking system should not be analyzed with a single score; instead, a comprehensive performance profile should be created.

The tracking community has started to investigate solutions for the aforementioned limitations. To address the detection-dependency problem and ameliorate the effect of noisy detections on tracking, Wen et al. [2015] proposed to evaluate data association and object detection jointly. They varied the detection threshold to generate detections corresponding to different values of precision and recall. Then, for each set of detections, they applied the data association method and computed the MOTA score. As a result, the MOTA scores corresponding to the precision-recall curve of the object detector form a 3D curve, which Wen et al. [2015] call the PR-MOTA

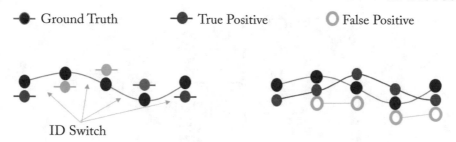

Figure 4.2: Example of the same MOTA score for two different tracking results, each preferable for a different application. The example contains only one ground-truth track (in five time steps), but two distinctive tracking results give the same MOTA score. The first result (left) shows five tracks, each of which can match to the ground truth but the length of each track is short. There are four identity switch errors so that the MOTA score is $1 - \frac{4}{5} = 0.2$. The second result (right) shows one perfect track (red) that matches the ground truth, but also contains two false alarm tracks. The MOTA score is again $1 - \frac{4}{5} = 0.2$. A multi-object tracking system that produces the first result rather than the second would be preferable for a crowd censusing application, but the MOTA score cannot distinguish the two. Conversely, if the task at hand is the analysis of trajectories, the second tracking system would be preferred over the first (because longer trajectories are expected, and the false alarms could be easily filtered out in a post-processing step, in this case, by track length). Again, since the MOTA score is the same for both tracking systems, it cannot be used to guide the selection of the appropriate system.

curve. An example of such a curve is shown in Fig. 4.3. Similar curves can be constructed for other traditional measures.

Using PR-MOTA curves, Wen et al. [2015] showed that the relative rankings of several state-of-the-art algorithms change depending on the output of the detector. The "best performance" is determined by a specific combination of the detection algorithm and the data association algorithm.

Similar ideas were proposed by Solera et al. [2015] whose evaluation approach generates synthetic detections through a controlled simulation of different degrees of detectors' reliability in terms of precision/recall and occlusions. Solera et al. [2015] designed protocols that modify the ground truth based on the desired false positive rate, miss rate, occlusion events, etc. The MOTA metric and another metric, called "track length," were then associated with each generated detection set. The final metric, similar to the area-under-curve, was used to integrate the evaluation results. In contrast to the work by Wen et al. [2015], which relies on the use of real detector output, applying synthetic detections enables one to analyze the robustness of a tracker with respect to one specific type of noise in the detection input, such as false detections or occlusions. Note, however, that in practice, systems users may still want to know what the best combination of real detector and tracker is.

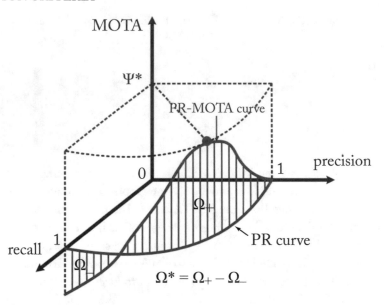

Figure 4.3: Illustration of a PR-MOTA curve. The purple curve is the classic precision-recall curve for object detection performance, while the red 3-D curve is the PR-MOTA curve $\mathcal{C} = \Psi(p, r)$, which describes detection and data association performance jointly. Metric value $\Psi^* = \arg\max_{\mathcal{C}} \Psi(p, r)$ describes the maximal MOTA score on the curve corresponding to the best performance. Metric value $\Omega^* = \int_{\mathcal{C}} \Psi(p, r) d\mathbf{s}$ describes the line integral along the curve, shown as the shaded area. The illustration is used with permission, courtesy of Longyin Wen, ©Longyin Wen.

An easily interpretable measure, called "mean time between failures (MTBF)," was recently proposed by Carr and Collins [2016] to help inspect the distribution of errorless durations of a tracking system. Trying to optimize this measure encourages an algorithm to produce long reliable tracks before it makes a mistake. This is in contrast to the traditional aggregation score MOTA, where a poor tracking algorithm can produce short tracks to avoid making additional mistakes and thus achieve a respectable MOTA score, as shown in Fig. 4.2.

To compute the MTBF score, one must first establish an association between ground truth and system-generated tracks. For each track, the periods of consistent identity assignment are counted from the run length encoding of its associated label sequence L: $RLE(L) = (R_1, R_2, ..., R_K)$, where $R_k = (l_k, D_k)$ is the k-th run with the label l_k repeated D_k times. The distribution of run lengths D_k from all the tracks provides a statistical measure of the tracking performance. The mean value, MTBF, for example, is the mean of the run lengths, whose associated label is a "true positive." False positives and negatives are not taken into account. A variant of this new measure is proven to be monotonic with respect to the three error sources: false positives, false negatives, and ID switches, which is an important property that guarantees a reduction in tracking error results in a better performance score.

Readers are reminded that tracking evaluation results reported in the literature may be inadvertently biased. While authors typically optimize the parameters of their new algorithm, they also typically give less attention to optimizing the parameters of competing algorithms. The statistical significance of performance differences on benchmarks is often not reported, and even if it exists, its practical implication may be negligible.

To better understand the performance of an algorithm, readers may want to compare results on test sequences with different attributes, e.g., complete or partial occlusions, scenes taken with a static vs. a moving camera, short or long sequences, etc. A useful reference in this regard is the evaluation protocol designed for single object tracking [Kristan et al., 2015, Wu et al., 2015].

Given the shortcomings of the evaluation criteria we here discussed, we expect a continuation of the recent research efforts to design evaluation protocols that fully test the robustness of a system and enable fair comparisons between competing solutions.

CHAPTER 5

Tracking with Multiple Cameras

The classic data association approaches we have discussed so far were originally designed to solve the *temporal* data association problem, that is, matching object measurements obtained at different times. It was assumed that objects are imaged through a single camera, and we relied on the notion of temporal smoothness to handle challenging tracking scenarios, such as occlusions or detector failure. The assumption of temporal smoothness for the motion or appearance of an object, however, is not always a valid assumption—the object could have abrupt change in its motion dynamics, or present a very different appearance due to pose, viewpoint, and lighting. How can we then handle these challenging tracking scenarios? A possible solution is to add sources of information by deploying multiple cameras with overlapping fields of view. This allows us to observe the objects from different viewpoints and apply fusion techniques to correct the errors that may occur in individual camera views. Using multiple views is advantageous because when an occlusion or detection error occurs in a certain view, it might not happen in other views.

With multiple cameras, the three-dimensional (3D) positions of moving objects can be estimated via homography or triangulation. Multi-view tracking can then assist in generating 3D trajectories of the motion of an object. Tracking multiple objects in several camera views is challenging because data association must be performed not only across time, as in single-view tracking, but also spatially, across views. We refer to the latter as the across-views or *spatial* data association problem.

Tracking errors in multiple views are made by automated tracking methods when the objects appear similar in the images and occur in dense groups, partially or completely occluding each other. In spatial data association, errors happen when image locations corresponding to different objects are mistakenly used to estimate 3D positions (see Fig. 5.1). Camera placement can reduce the potential occurrence of data association errors by imposing appropriate geometric constraints on the triangulation.

Two strategies can be used to solve the multi-object multi-view tracking task that differ in the order of the association processes: The "reconstruction-tracking approach" processes the across-view associations first by reconstructing the 3D positions of candidate measurements (Sec. 5.1). It then matches the 3D positions to previously established object tracks. The "tracking-reconstruction approach" processes the across-time associations first and establishes 2D objects

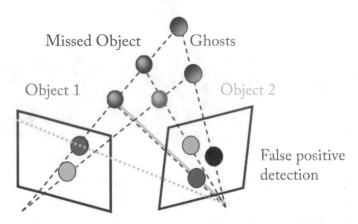

Figure 5.1: If objects 1 and 2 are matched correctly across views (green to green and brown to brown), triangulation yields their correct 3D positions. Epipolar geometry supports this matching process: Here the ray from the right camera view of object 1 to its 3D position (solid yellow line) is imaged in the left camera view as an epipolar line (dashed yellow line) through the image of object 1. If the false positive detection in the right view (blue) is erroneously matched with the projection of objects 1 or 2 in the left view (green or brown), a "ghost" point (blue sphere) is triangulated. Note also that due to occlusion, a third object (red) will be entirely missed.

tracks for each view. It then reconstructs 3D motion trajectories using the matched 2D tracks (Sec. 5.2).

Each approach has its advantages and disadvantages, especially in imaging scenarios where objects appear in dense groups, look similar, and are thus difficult to distinguish. In the literature, the two schemes have been compared for analysis of human motion [Li et al., 2002, Tyagi et al., 2007b] and animal flight [Wu et al., 2009b]. Typically the reconstruction-tracking scheme is favored [Dockstader and Tekalp, 2001, Eshel and Moses, 2008, Fleuret et al., 2008, Khan and Shah, 2006, Li et al., 2002, Liu et al., 2012, Mittal and Davis, 2003, Otsuka and Mukawa, 2004, Tyagi et al., 2007b] but not for all applications [Zarrabeitia et al., 2014] .

Finally, spatial data association for uncalibrated cameras is possible if the motion of objects is restricted on a surface [Felsberg et al., 2013]. Some work addresses tracking objects in a camera network with non-overlapping fields of view. Establishing across-view correspondence in this context is known as the re-identification problem. Methods that address this problem try to build discriminant object descriptors and utilize the topology of the camera network for re-entry prediction [Doretto et al., 2011, Erdem and Sclaroff, 2012, Kang et al., 2005, Song and Roy-Chowdhury, 2008]. To learn about these methods, we refer interested readers to the companion book by Roy-Chowdhury and Song [2011] in this publication series. We focus on cameras with overlapping fields of view in this chapter.

5.1   THE RECONSTRUCTION-TRACKING APPROACH

The reconstruction-tracking approach can be seen as a feature-to-feature fusion process [Tyagi et al., 2007a], where the features are 3D object positions processed from 2D image measurements. Tracking in 3D is a reasonable choice if the 3D positions of objects or object features can be estimated accurately. If the information about an object gathered from several rather than only two camera views is fused and the cameras are spatially calibrated, the 3D position estimates can typically be made quite accurately within the calibration volume (Fig. 5.2). Obtaining *accurate* position estimates, however, is not the main challenge of multi-object multi-view tracking; instead, the main challenge is the correct interpretation of *ambiguous* position estimates, which are caused by occlusion or missed detection [Keck and Davis, 2011]. Such ambiguity becomes significantly worse when correspondences need to be established for tracking dense crowds of objects.

The first step of a typical reconstruction-tracking approach is the 3D estimation of object positions based on across-view matching of 2D object measurements. When objects of interest move on a planar surface, the complexity of the across-view matching is relatively simpler. The 2D object measurement from each camera view can be re-mapped to the world plane by estimating a homography mapping. The "ground plane assumption" is commonly used by pedestrian tracking applications [Eshel and Moses, 2008, Fleuret et al., 2008, Khan and Shah, 2006, Mittal and Davis, 2003].

In the more general scenario where objects move in free 3D space, the across-view matching process can be facilitated by an understanding of epipolar geometry (Fig. 5.3). For a given 3D point, an epipolar line in one view is defined as the projection of a ray emanating from the center of projection in the other view and passing through this 3D point. If a 3D object is visible in the first view and the multi-camera system is well calibrated, its 2D image must appear on this epipolar line. If inaccuracies in camera calibration or 2D position estimates occur, the object projection appears at least near the epipolar line (Fig. 5.4). Once the matching is established, triangulation is used to "reconstruct" the 3D object position from the 2D measurements.

The efficacy of the reconstruction process is highly dependent on the correct matching of 2D measurements. Fortunately, a test can be applied to check if 2D measurements of different objects are falsely used to triangulate the 3D position of an object. This test re-projects the computed 3D position into each camera view and compares the 2D position of the reprojection with the original 2D measurements. If the root mean squared distance between the 2D measurements and the 2D reprojections, also called the "reconstruction residual" or "reprojection error," is deemed small, the across-view association of the 2D measurements is considered reliable. However, ambiguity may still remain even if the reconstruction residual is small. More cameras are advantageous to avoid ambiguity in across-view associations of 2D measurements. In particular, the use of three cameras, instead of two, in a non-collinear configuration leads to reduced data association errors (Fig. 5.2).

The second step of a reconstruction-tracking approach is the tracking step, which requires across-time data association. Accordingly, techniques from previous chapters apply. The tracking

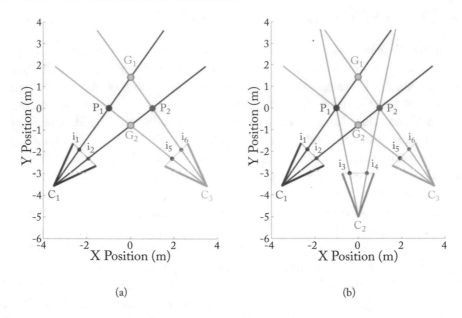

(a)   (b)

Figure 5.2: Two vs. three cameras. (a) In this two-camera system, 2D data points i_1 and i_5 should be matched to reconstruct the 3D position of P_1 (purple), and i_2 and i_6 to reconstruct P_2 (blue). A data association error occurs when i_1 and i_6 are used to reconstruct 3D "ghost point" G_1, and i_2 and i_5 to reconstruct G_2. (b) With the addition of a third camera, these data association errors can be avoided because the 2D data points i_3 and i_4 are consistent with the 3D points P_1 and P_2 and not with the ghost points.

step can be performed in 3D, using the estimated 3D positions [Eshel and Moses, 2008, Fleuret et al., 2008, Khan and Shah, 2006, Liu et al., 2012, Mittal and Davis, 2003, Otsuka and Mukawa, 2004, Tyagi et al., 2007b], or in 2D by tracking the 2D projections of reconstructed 3D points into the image plane of each camera [Dockstader and Tekalp, 2001, Li et al., 2002].

For objects moving in 3D space, Wu et al. [2009b] applied the multi-dimensional assignment formulation with epipolar geometry constraints to solve both the across-view and across-time data associations. Instead of making a hard decision at each time step, Liu et al. [2012] proposed a multiple hypothesis generation and verification mechanism to resolve the ambiguity in the across-view association step. Another interesting across-view association approach was proposed by Otsuka and Mukawa [2004] to explicitly model the occlusion process given accurate camera geometry information. Instead of using a 3D point estimate, silhouettes of objects were extracted and visual cones were constructed to represent a measurement. A variant of Multiple Hypothesis Tracking was adapted to predict when and how an occlusion event was going to happen. However, such an approach is only applicable in highly controlled environments with sufficient coverage of overlapping fields of view from many different viewpoints.

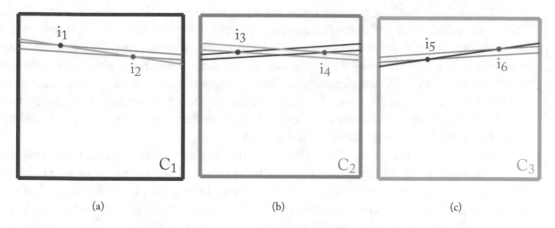

(a)   (b)   (c)

Figure 5.3: Epipolar lines in a three-camera system. The rays through 3D object positions P_1 and P_2 shown in Figure 5.2 B appear as epipolar lines in the three camera views. For example, in camera C1, image points i_1 and i_2 appear at the intersections of the epipolar lines that arise from projections of rays through camera C2 (yellow) and camera C3 (green).

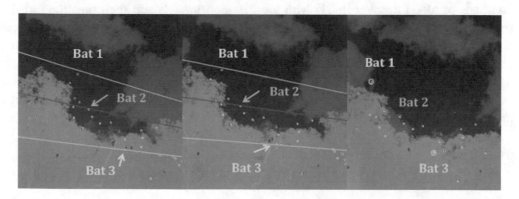

Figure 5.4: The bats detected in the rightmost view are imaged in the other camera views on or near the respective epipolar lines.

5.2   THE TRACKING-RECONSTRUCTION APPROACH

The tracking-reconstruction approach can be interpreted as a track-to-track fusion process that benefits from deferring assignment decisions, as in Multiple Hypothesis Tracking. When information about the 2D track is accumulated over time, the ambiguity in matching tracks across views becomes smaller. The method is suitable when a distributed system architecture is required to prevent "one-point-failures," which may occur in a centralized system used by the reconstruction-tracking method.

The goal of a tracking-reconstruction approach is to match 2D tracks across camera views. Tracks, also called "tracklets" in the literature, carry richer information than a single measurement. One complication is that the correspondence of tracks across views is usually not one-to-one. A long 2D track in one view may correspond to several short tracks in another view. In the most challenging case, an object may be occluded in each camera view at some point in time, leading to the occurrence of track fragments in each view. The timing of the occlusion is typically not the same in any two views. This means that the 2D tracks in different views that correspond to the same object usually have different start and end times.

To match the 2D tracks with different length, Wu et al. [2009b] first break long tracks into short tracklets so that candidate tracklets to be matched are aligned in time. Tracklets are then matched in a greedy way where each tracklet can be matched multiple times. The resulting matched 2D tracklets are reconstructed into 3D trajectory pieces that are then linked into complete 3D trajectories. The method was tested on infrared video sequences of emerging bats at "medium" density, and was shown to be effective to reduce the "ghost effect," which is the occurance of an incorrect triangulation from the misassociation across views (see Fig. 5.1).

Zarrabeitia et al. [2014] also developed a technique to reconstruct the three-dimensional trajectories of blood droplets using a tracking-reconstruction approach. Their approach tracks hundreds of blood droplets in 2D with local motion models and then uses the individual 2D tracks to learn a global motion model. This model can be used to estimate the 3D positions of the blood droplets. The 2D tracks are matched across views as continuous paths rather than sequences of discrete 2D positions. This approach is powerful because it minimizes the impact of any noise in the measurements of these 2D positions as well as inaccuracies in the synchronization of the cameras. Interestingly, the 3D droplet paths can even be estimated from the videos of a set of unsynchronized cameras.

5.3   AN EXAMPLE OF SPATIAL DATA ASSOCIATION

In this section, we describe a spatial (across-view) data association method based on a variant of Multiple Hypothesis Tracking (see Sec. 2.5), known as the multi-dimensional assignment formulation [Poore, 1994, Wu et al., 2009b]. The inputs to this method are the lists of measurements from each camera in a multi-camera imaging system, along with camera calibration information. The output is the set of correspondence across views that assigns measurements to a common object or background clutter. This method may serve as a first step in a reconstruction-tracking approach.

Formally, we define the state $\mathbf{x}$ of an object of interest by its position in 3D space. The measurement returned by a proper detection method is a 2D point observation of an object on the image plane or a false alarm. Given K calibrated and synchronized cameras that share overlapping fields of view and n_k measurements in the field of view of camera k, the state $\mathbf{x}_o$ of an object of interest o and its observations $z_{k,o}$ can be related according to the equation

$$z_{k,o} = H_k \, \mathbf{x}_o + w_k, \quad \text{for } k = 1, ..., K, \; o = 1, ..., N; \tag{5.1}$$

where w_k is zero-mean Gaussian noise process with covariance R_k, and H_k is the projection matrix for camera k. Each point measurement z_{k,o_k} is either the projection of some object o in camera k plus additive Gaussian noise $\mathcal{N}(0, R_k)$, or a false-positive detection, which is assumed to occur uniformly likely within the field of view of camera k.

For each camera, we define the probability for an object to be detected to be $P_{D_k} < 1$. We add "dummy" measurements $z_{k,0}$ to handle the case of missed detections, accordingly. We use the notation $Z_{i_1 i_2 ... i_K}$ to indicate that the measurements $z_{1,i_1}, z_{2,i_2}, \ldots, z_{K,i_K}$ originate from a common object in the scene. The likelihood that $Z_{i_1 i_2 ... i_K}$ describes object state $\mathbf{x}_o$ is given as

$$p(Z_{i_1 i_2 ... i_K} | \mathbf{x}_o) \;=\; \prod_{k=1}^{K} \{ [1 - P_{D_k}]^{1 - u(i_k)} \times [P_{D_k} \, p(z_{k,i_k} | \mathbf{x}_o)]^{u(i_k)} \} \tag{5.2}$$

where $u(i_k)$ is an indicator function defined as 0 if $i_k = 0$ and 1 otherwise. The conditional probability density of a measurement z_{k,i_k} originating from object o, is

$$p(z_{k,i_k} | \mathbf{x}_o) = \mathcal{N}(z_{k,i_k}; H_k \, \mathbf{x}_o, R_s). \tag{5.3}$$

The likelihood that $Z_{i_1 i_2 ... i_K}$ is unrelated to object o or related to dummy object $\oslash$ is

$$p(Y_{i_1 i_2 ... i_K} | \oslash) = \prod_{k=1}^{K} [\frac{1}{V_k}]^{u(i_k)}, \tag{5.4}$$

where V_k is the volume of the field of view of camera k. Since we do not know the true state $\mathbf{x}_o$, we replace it with a least-square solution using multiview geometry. If we assume each measurement z_{k,i_k} is expressed as image coordinates (u_k, v_k) and the state of the object in 3D is expressed as a homogeneous coordinate $\mathbf{x} = (x, y, z, 1)^T$, then for each measurement there are two linear constraints:

$$\begin{cases} u_k (H_k^{(3)} \mathbf{x}) - H_k^{(1)} = 0 \\ v_k (H_k^{(3)} \mathbf{x}) - H_k^{(2)} = 0 \end{cases} \tag{5.5}$$

where $H_k^{(i)}$ is the i-th row of matrix H_k. To find the least squared solution $\hat{\mathbf{x}}$, the Direct Linear Transformation (DLT) method [Hartley and Zisserman, 2003] solves the overdetermined linear system in Eq. (5.5) with $2K$ constraints.

We now can define the cost of associating the K-tuple $Z_{i_1 i_2 \ldots i_K}$ to object o as the negative log-likelihood ratio:

$$
\begin{aligned}
c_{i_1 i_2 \ldots i_K} &= -\ln \frac{p\left(Z_{i_1 i_2 \ldots i_K} \mid o\right)}{p\left(Z_{i_1 i_2 \ldots i_K} \mid \oslash\right)} \\
&= \sum_{k=1}^{K}\left\{[u(i_k) - 1]\ln(1 - \mathrm{P}_{D_k}) - u(i_k)\ln\left(\frac{\mathrm{P}_{D_k} V_k}{|2\pi R_k|^{1/2}}\right)\right. \\
&\quad \left. + u(i_k)[\frac{1}{2}(z_{k,i_k} - H_k\hat{\mathbf{x}}_o)^T R_k^{-1}(z_{k,i_k} - H_k\hat{\mathbf{x}}_o)]\right\}
\end{aligned}
\tag{5.6}
$$

We use the binary variable $z_{i_1 i_2 \ldots i_K}$ to indicate if $Z_{i_1 i_2 \ldots i_K}$ is associated with a candidate object or not. Assuming that such associations are independent, our goal is to find the most likely set of K-tuples that minimizes the linear cost function:

$$
\min \sum_{i_1=0}^{n_1} \sum_{i_2=0}^{n_2} \cdots \sum_{i_K=0}^{n_K} c_{i_1 i_2 \ldots i_K}\, x_{i_1 i_2 \ldots i_K}
\tag{5.7}
$$

$$
\text{s. t. } \sum_{i_2=0}^{n_2} \sum_{i_3=0}^{n_3} \cdots \sum_{i_K=0}^{n_K} x_{i_1 i_2 \ldots i_K} = 1; \quad i_1 = 1, 2, \ldots, n_1
$$

$$
\sum_{i_1=0}^{n_1} \sum_{i_3=0}^{n_3} \cdots \sum_{i_K=0}^{n_K} x_{i_1 i_2 \ldots i_K} = 1; \quad i_2 = 1, 2, \ldots, n_2
$$

$$
\vdots
$$

$$
\sum_{i_1=0}^{n_1} \sum_{i_2=0}^{n_2} \cdots \sum_{i_{K-1}=0}^{n_{K-1}} x_{i_1 i_2 \ldots i_K} = 1; \quad i_K = 1, 2, \ldots, n_K.
$$

The equality constraints imply every measurement except for the dummy placeholder has to be explained and the matching is one-to-one between real measurements. Each measurement is either assigned to some object or claimed to be a false-positive detection.

Equation 5.7 is known as a generalized multidimensional assignment problem, which is NP-hard when the dimension $K \geq 3$. It can be seen as finding a weighted maximum matching on a hypergraph, where a hyperedge must connect more than two vertices at the same time. Therefore, it is a generalization of bipartite matching (see Sec. 2.3) The processing time for the optimal solution is unacceptable in dense tracking scenarios, even if a branch-and-bound search method is used, because such a method is inevitably enumerative in nature. The alternative is to search for a sub-optimal solution to this combinatorial problem, using a greedy approach [Robertson, 2001] or Lagrangian relaxation [Deb et al., 1997, Poore and Robertson, 1997]. The popular semi-definite programming (SDP) technique was adopted by Shafique et al. [2008] who relaxed the original discrete optimization to a rank-constrained continuous optimization. An iterative Lagrange relaxation procedure was applied by Deb et al. [1997] to the dual problem. The procedure halted its iterations when the duality gap was sufficiently small. Here we briefly outline a greedy randomized adaptive search procedure (GRASP) [Robertson, 2001, Wu, 2012], which randomly selects a greedy solution as a starting point and performs local search in feasible solution space.

GRASP consists of a randomized greedy step and a local search step at each iteration. In the randomized greedy step, a restricted candidate list is constructed greedily from the remaining feasible assignments, from which an assignment is selected randomly and added to the solution set. In the local search step, the so-called two-assignment-exchange operation is performed between real measurement assignments. That is, for two tuples $Z_{i_1 \ldots i_j \ldots i_K}$ and $Z_{i'_1 \ldots i'_j \ldots i'_K}$ from the feasible solution, we exchange the assignment to $Z_{i_1 \ldots i'_j \ldots i_K}$ and $Z_{i'_1 \ldots i_j \ldots i'_K}$ if such an operation decreases the total cost in Eq. (5.7). The tuples and their indices to exchange are selected to be the most profitable pair at the current iteration. The exchange takes place recursively until no exchange can be made anymore. Details of the GRASP implementation and other possible greedy constructions and assignment exchange strategies can be found in the work by Robertson [2001].

In practice, a technique similar to "gating" (see Sec. 2.2) during the initialization step is performed to reduce the number of possible tuples as follows. Given a pair of calibrated views, we establish the correspondence of the two projected images of an object using epipolar geometry. Thus, we only need to evaluate the candidate tuples that lie within the neighborhood of corresponding epipolar lines. Specifically, all candidate points from the second view that can be matched to a 2D point z (expressed in homogeneous coordinates) in the first view should be on the epipolar line computed by Fz, where F is the fundamental matrix that captures the geometric relationship between two cameras [Hartley and Zisserman, 2003]. A user-defined threshold is adopted to prune candidate points that are far away from this line so the total possible number of pairings can be reduced significantly.

5.4   DISCUSSION

Readers might be aware that finding the across-view correspondence is a fundamental problem in stereo vision and "structure-from-motion." For stereo matching, the goal is to provide dense correspondences for every pixel in the image so that a dense 3D reconstruction can be carried out. For structure-from-motion, an important step is to establish the correspondences between key points from the images using some similarity measure of local patch descriptors. The correspondences provide constraints on the relative camera poses so that the motion, defined by the "extrinsic parameters," can be computed.

The spatial data association problem discussed in the context of multi-object multi-view tracking here is different. It is a sparse correspondence problem, as opposed to the dense matching problem in stereo vision. If two objects are far apart in 3D space, their projections, two measurements, may or may not be close in camera views. This implies a common *smoothness* assumption in data association of neighboring pixels for dense surface reconstruction does not naturally apply in the tracking scenario.

The across-view key-point correspondence problem in the structure-from-motion pipeline also requires a solution to a sparse problem. Here the task is to compute the camera motion. In the tracking problem, the system of cameras has been calibrated. Also, key points are typically not required to be matched exhaustively and exclusively, so each key point does not compete in the matching process. Therefore there is no need to optimize a cost function to resolve matching uncertainty.

In challenging tracking scenarios where similar objects are closely spaced and form a dense group, it is very difficult to identify correct correspondences across views or across time. Both "reconstruction-tracking" and "tracking-reconstruction" methods can make mistakes in solving their first association sub-problem, and errors are then propagated to the second association sub-problem. Enforcing a sequential order of association sub-problems is not an optimal algorithmic design. We may design a global formulation to jointly solve both sub-problems at the same time. Such a formulation has to deal with the compounded complexity of exponential growth of data association hypotheses, since each sub-problem is already a computationally hard problem. Early efforts to approach this direction of research propose to operate on small fragments of tracks using a "tracklet linking process" [Attanasi et al., 2015]. We will explain the tracklet linking problem in the next chapter. For a general discussion on multi-sensor fusion in tracking, we also refer readers to the extensive work in the radar literature [Bar-Shalom and Li, 1995, Mahler, 2014] that is built on top of the probabilistic data association methods we have explained in Chapter 2.

CHAPTER 6

The Tracklet Linking Approach

This chapter describes the problem of matching trajectory segments, also called tracklets. Trajectory segmentation occurs due to occlusion or misassociation and can be addressed in a batch process. The tracklet linking problem is a generalization of the traditional data association problem that involves single observations and aims to match measurements to measurements, or measurements to already established tracks. Each tracklet typically carries much more information than the single measurements considered in the previous chapters (e.g., centroid positions). Data association ambiguity can be resolved by optimizing a cost function that considers the smoothness of object motion and appearance over several frames. With this approach, tracklets may be stitched together and full trajectories thus recovered. The tracklet stitching approach can be applied to both single-view and multi-view settings [Wu et al., 2011b].

The advantages of using tracklets are twofold. First, as we have already seen, the complexity of most data association methods usually grows quickly when many frames are processed in a batch mode. By matching tracklets, especially long tracklets, the time span of the sequence in a batch that a system can handle typically increases significantly. Second, each tracklet already carries filtered information and, therefore, the descriptor for each tracklet is much more informative than a simple instantaneous measurement can be [Bak et al., 2012, Raptis and Soatto, 2010].

6.1   REVIEW OF EXISTING WORK

Static scene occlusions or inter-object occlusions are the main causes that break a complete trajectory into pieces. In order to stitch pieces that occur before and after occlusion events, a common assumption is adopted in track linking that a complete track should obey certain smoothness properties, either in its appearance or motion. Most existing techniques that work with tracklets simply extend a measurement-to-measurement association method by redesigning the similarity function under the same mathematical framework, such as the 2D assignment problem [Cai and Medioni, 2014, Henriques et al., 2011, Huang et al., 2008, Perera et al., 2006, Singh et al., 2008, Song and Roy-Chowdhury, 2008], MCMC sampling [Ge and Collins, 2008], network-flow optimization [Castañón and Finn, 2011, Wang et al., 2014a, Wu et al., 2011b], or generalized linear assignment [Dicle et al., 2013].

Instead of organizing temporal data-association hierarchically, where, at each level, *local* links between track fragments are produced [Andriluka et al., 2008, Huang et al., 2008, Perera et al., 2006, Xing et al., 2009], Nillius et al. [2006] solved the problem *globally* by processing the track graph that represented all object interactions. Their method used the "junction-tree algorithm" for loopy graph inference to maintain track identities. Unfortunately, the size of the state space defined for each node in the graph that models object interaction grows exponentially as the number of objects involved in the interaction increases. Since the state space, i.e., the permutation space over the object identities, is large, their method has to incorporate some heuristics to make it practical, especially when objects interaction is frequent. A similar track graph was adopted by Wu et al. [2011b] who reformulated the task of global tracklet linking as a set-cover problem. This permits the use of a relatively easier greedy algorithm that solves the problem with a theoretically guaranteed approximation quality. The same idea was also extended to link tracklets in a multi-view scenario, where tracklets are generated from different camera views.

Tracklet linking plays an important role for biomedical image analysis tasks, such as cell lineage reconstruction in time-lapse microscopy [Li et al., 2008a]. Due to frequent interactions, highly nonrigid deformations, and cluttered background, it is not easy to develop a robust low-level tracker for these image sequences. An additional linking procedure must be performed that exploits the spatial-temporal context. An interesting problem under consideration in the biomedical domain is how to identify mitosis events where living cells undergo splitting as a physical process. Bise et al. [2011] proposed to generate short reliable tracklets of cells and to form tree structures to represent when a mother cell divides into two daughter cells. With that, they solved the global tracklet association for the tree structures by linear programming.

Track linking methods typically compare features extracted from tracklets to decide if a stitch should be made. The methods can be categorized according to the "local" or "global" nature of the features. The feature is *local* if it only represents the information carried within the tracklet under consideration. The feature is *global* if it depends on the whole trajectory formed by **all** the tracklets along the path. Most previous track linking methods use local features only. The use of a global feature is more appropriate if a stitch requires evaluation of the whole set of tracklets that form the trajectory at a given point in time.

Previous track linking efforts can be categorized according to their stitching strategy which either follows a non-iterative or an iterative process. For a typical iterative process, tracklets are linked as a pair at each iteration, and the complete path is formed incrementally [Huang et al., 2008, Li et al., 2008a, Perera et al., 2006, Wu et al., 2011b, Xing et al., 2009]. For a non-iterative process, a global optimization problem is formulated, whose solution provides all the paths at the same time [Bise et al., 2011, Castañón and Finn, 2011, Dicle et al., 2013, Nillius et al., 2006, Wang et al., 2014a, Wu et al., 2011b].

6.2   AN EXAMPLE OF TRACKLET LINKING USING A TRACK GRAPH

In this section, we give an example of a tracklet linking framework that helps resolve uncertainty in data association due to object interactions or mutual occlusions. The framework is based on a graph representation, the aforementioned *track graph*. Formally, a track graph $\mathbf{G} = (V, E)$ is defined over sets of vertices V that represent individual or merged tracks and edges E that represent merging or splitting events. A merged track is produced when multiple objects are treated as a single group due to either a close interaction between objects or an overlapped projection of moving objects in 3D space. The directed edge $e_{i,j}$ from vertex v_i to v_j represents that track v_i is merged with track v_j if v_j is a merged track, or that v_i is split to track v_j if v_i is a merged track, as shown in Fig. 6.1.

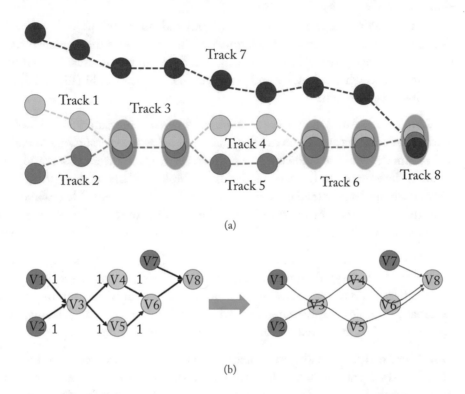

Figure 6.1: A tracking example that consists of three interacting objects and eight system-generated tracks (a) and the corresponding track graph (b). The track graph represents two objects that occlude each other for a while, then move apart, then merge again, and finally interact with a third object. The number on the edge shows the number of objects involved in the track. The track graph is particularly useful to visualize such frequent track-merging and track-splitting events. The task of the linking algorithms is to process the track graph (b-left) and produce the resolved graph (b-right), where each red arrow connects multiple vertices (i.e., tracks) and maintains the identity of the tracked object.

For simplicity, we assume each individual track is part of a complete trajectory corresponding to a true object, but the number of objects is unknown. The *flow* on the edge indicates how many objects are involved during the merging or splitting event. The vertex that has only incoming edges is called *sink*; the vertex that has only outgoing edges is called *source*. The set of all source vertices is denoted by S, and the set of all sink vertices by T. Each vertex has its *track-capacity* to represent single or multiple objects. For a source vertex, its associated track-capacity is the sum of outgoing flows; for a sink vertex, its associated track-capacity is the sum of incoming flows; for other intermediate vertices, the sum of incoming flows is equal to the sum of outgoing flows for balance. For tracking in a single view, an isolated vertex that has no incoming or outgoing edges has capacity one. We remove these isolated vertices in preprocessing, as they do not require occlusion reasoning.

Similar to the methods by Perera et al. [2006] and Bose et al. [2007], a forward-backward process is performed to construct a track graph. It first processes the sequence forward in time to generate basic tracks with a low-level tracker and merge hypotheses. It then goes backward to break some tracks when necessary and generate split hypotheses. Finally it defines the vertices and edges of the track graph.

1. **Tracking Forward:** A new tracker is initiated when a measurement cannot be associated with an existing tracker. Each existing tracker chooses the measurement nearest to its position estimate, which is predicted by a Kalman filter, as its current observation. If a measurement is determined to be associated with multiple trackers, each of these trackers terminates itself, and a new tracker is initiated for this measurement. Meanwhile, a track-merge hypothesis H_m is generated and added to the list of hypotheses. An existing tracker also terminates itself if it is not associated with any measurement for a certain number of frames.

2. **Tracking Backward:** If a track is not initiated within the entrance zone of the scene (e.g., the image boundary), then it must be a track that is split from a previously merged track. Its position is predicted backward in time to find a nearest measurement. The track that originally occupies this measurement is denoted as a merged track. Meanwhile, a track split hypothesis H_s is generated and added to the list of hypotheses.

3. **Building Track Graph:** The list of merge/split hypotheses is sorted according to time. A vertex of the track graph is created for each track on this list. For each merge hypothesis H_m that merges track $\mathcal{T}_{i_1}, \mathcal{T}_{i_2}, ...\mathcal{T}_{i_m}$ to track $\mathcal{T}_j$, corresponding edges from vertices $v_{i_1}, v_{i_2}, ..., v_{i_m}$ to v_j are added to the track graph. For each split hypothesis H_s that splits track $\mathcal{T}_i$ into track $\mathcal{T}_{j_1}, \mathcal{T}_{j_2}, ...\mathcal{T}_{j_n}$, the corresponding edges from vertex v_i to $v_{j_1}, v_{j_2}, ..., v_{j_n}$ are added. Optionally, the track capacity of each node can be determined by solving a minimum-flow problem where the lower bound on the capacity of each edge is one. This can be achieved efficiently by iteratively searching for a "reducing path" (as opposed to the "augmenting path" in the max-flow Ford-Fulkerson method [Cormen et al., 1990]) and updating the residual networks.

There are several linking strategies that can be applied to the track graph. If occlusion occurs for a short period of time or the local feature computed from each tracklet is sufficiently discriminant, we can use a local linking strategy that connects pairs of tracklets at a time. The optimization problem can be cast as the 2D assignment or network flow formulation introduced in Sec. 3.2. Details on applicable linking strategies were explained by Wu et al. [2011b]. If occlusion occurs frequently for a long period of time or a global feature needs to be computed to describe the whole trajectory, a global linking strategy can be applied, which may connect several trajectory segments together at the same time, and the cost along a flow path is not decomposable. The problem can be converted into a weighted set-cover problem as follows.

For a given track graph, we enumerate all possible paths from source set S to sink set T, where each path consists of a sequence $\{v_{i_1} v_{i_1} ... v_{i_p}\}$ of vertices visited. To connect the formulation to the standard set-cover problem, we ignore the order between the vertices of the sequences. The set of all paths is denoted as P. A weight w_p is associated with a path p that measures the negative log-likelihood of the path being a true trajectory, or equivalently the "cost" of the path based on a global feature such as motion smoothness. The objective function then is defined as selecting a subset P' of P such that the sum of the costs of all selected paths is minimum. Each vertex $v \in V$ has to be on some path at least once. Mathematically, this is equivalent to the following linear integer programming problem, where x_p is an integer variable to indicate if path p is selected x_p times:

$$\min \sum_{p \in P} w_p x_p$$

$$\text{s. t.} \quad \sum_{p:v \in p} x_p \geq 1, \quad \forall v \in V$$

$$x_p \geq 0 \text{ and } x_p \text{ is integer.} \tag{6.1}$$

To solve the set-cover problem, the deterministic greedy method achieves an approximation ratio of $\mathcal{H}(s)$, where s is the size of the largest set, and $\mathcal{H}(n) = \sum_{i=1}^{n} 1/i \approx \log(n)$ is the n-th harmonic number [Lovasz, 1975].

A more general scenario of track linking is to link tracklets from multiple views with a global linking cost. For ease of notation, we here consider only two views, but the method can be extended to an arbitrary number of views. We formulate the multi-view global linking problem as a *joint*-set-cover problem. Specifically, we generate a track graph for each view independently as $G_1 = (V_1, E_1)$ and $G_2 = (V_2, E_2)$. For each graph G_i, $i = 1, 2$, we enumerate all valid paths in set P_i. We define a_p and b_q to measure the respective likelihoods of paths $p \in P_1$ and $q \in P_2$ being true trajectories. Our goal is to choose a subset $P'_i \subseteq P_i$ to achieve a cover on V_i for each view, subject to the additional constraint that enforces any selected path $p \in P'_i$ has a corresponding path $q \in P'_j$ with an across-view matching cost $c_{p,q}$. We seek the solution that achieves the minimum weighted sum. The problem can be formulated as the following linear integer programming problem, where $z_{p,q}$ is a binary variable to indicate if a path pair (p, q), $p \in P_1$ and $q \in P_2$, is selected or not:

$$\min \sum_p a_p \sum_q z_{p,q} + \sum_q b_q \sum_p z_{p,q} + \sum_p \sum_q c_{p,q} z_{p,q}$$

$$\text{s. t.} \quad \sum_{p:u \in p} \sum_q z_{p,q} \geq 1, \forall u \in V_1,$$

$$\sum_{q:v \in q} \sum_p z_{p,q} \geq 1, \forall v \in V_2,$$

$$z_{p,q} \geq 0 \text{ and } z_{p,q} \text{ is integer.} \tag{6.2}$$

It is easy to see that the joint-set-cover problem defined in Eq. (6.2) can be reduced to a standard weighted set-cover problem, with a proof given by Wu et al. [2011b]. In case some object does not appear in the field of a particular view, e.g., set $p \in P_1$ has no matching set $q \in P_2$, we add all pairs (p, q_0) to the joint set O, where $p \in P_1$ and q_0 is a "dummy" placeholder, and assign a large matching cost so that these elements have a low priority of being selected.

To test the scalability and robustness of various linking methods, we here show a quantitative evaluation on synthetic data. Results on real world video sequences were reported by Wu et al. [2011b]. To set up the simulation experiment, we randomly generated colored spheres with 10-unit radii, moving at a constant speed in a 500^3-unit 3D space. Each sphere carries a unique color as its label, and the arrival time of each sphere is drawn uniformly from the interval $[1, T_{\max}]$ with $T_{\max} = 250$ frames. We created two virtual cameras for viewing the spheres from directions differing by 45°. The motion model of each sphere is $X^{(t)} = FX^{(t-1)} + W^{(t)}$ and $Z^{(t)} = HX^{(t)} + V^{(t)}$ with a 6D state X (3D position and 3D velocity), 2D observation Z (virtual view of sphere), state transition matrix F, projection matrix H, and zero-mean Gaussian noise processes W and V with respective covariance matrices diag$(1, 1, 1, 0.1, 0.1, 0.1)$, and diag$(1, 1)$. We generated six datasets (D1–D6) with increasing density, roughly characterizing "sparse," "medium," and "dense" tracking scenarios. Each dataset contains five sequences, each with 250 frames per view, resulting in a total of 15,000 test frames. Key statistics of the synthetic data are summarized in Table 6.1.

The track graph representation for the simulation data was constructed by the forward-backward process described earlier. We evaluated five tracklet linking methods, including local linking, network linking, global linking, multiview linking [Wu et al., 2011b], and the Dynamic Bayesian Network (DBN) method [Nillius et al., 2006]. Both local linking and network linking connect tracklets that only use a pairwise matching cost, while the other three linking methods depend on a global matching cost. The global-linking method uses the set-cover formulation explained above, and the multiview linking uses the joint-set-cover formulation. All linking methods use the same set of tracklets from the track graph as input. For the local-linking method, the cost of pairing two tracklets was chosen to be the standard deviation of the linear-regression residual over the observed 2D coordinates, assuming that the motion is along a straight line for short periods. In case a long tracklet may present nonlinear motion pattern, we only extracted at most 10 measurements right before or after interactions. For the global-linking method, the cost function that measures how likely several tracklets can form a smooth trajectory was evaluated by Kalman smoothing. For the multi-view linking method, the across-view cost function was defined as the reconstruction error according to the epipolar geometry, which is a least-square solution to the triangulation. In our implementation of the dynamic Bayesian network method by Nillius et al. [2006], we followed their recommendation to restrict the dependence between two vertices (here the number of objects involved in an occlusion event and the frequency of such events) within 20 frames. Details of the heuristics can be found in the paper by Nillius et al. [2006].

Table 6.1: Statistics of synthetic datasets and CLEAR MOTA results for comparison

	Datasets with Increasing Object Density					
	D1	**D2**	**D3**	**D4**	**D5**	**D6**
Avg. Objs / frame	8.8	17.8	27.1	36.2	45.45	54.6
Max. Objs / frame	16	27	38	51	59	73
Occlusions / frame	0.13	0.60	1.53	2.69	3.87	5.48
	Results (MOTA)					
Nillius et al. [2006]	0.92	**0.92**	0.86	0.82	NA	NA
Local Linking	0.90	0.83	0.75	0.68	0.59	0.53
Network Linking	**0.95**	0.91	0.87	0.82	0.81	0.80
Global Linking	**0.95**	**0.92**	**0.89**	**0.85**	**0.83**	**0.81**
Multiview Linking	**0.95**	**0.92**	**0.89**	**0.85**	0.81	0.78

We measured the performance of each linking method using the CLEAR MOTA evaluation measure described in Chapter 4 and here present the results in Table 6.1. Not surprisingly, the performance for all methods decreased as the density of objects in the scene increased. Both the global- and multiview-linking methods outperformed the other linking strategies. The method by Nillius et al. [2006], also a global approach, achieved comparable performance but failed to handle very dense scenarios (no reports for D5, D6). The method is simply too slow because its state space is too large even with their proposed heuristics applied [Nillius et al., 2006]. For a vertex with n incoming and n outgoing edges, our global-linking method enumerated n^2 paths passing this vertex. In contrast, the method by Nillius et al. [2006] must evaluate $n!$ possibilities of matching between incoming and outgoing edges.

Although the multiview-linking method showed a good performance by using additional 3D geometric information, it started to degrade in the dense scenarios of our simulation (D5, D6), where the size of the proposed joint-set cover problem became much larger than each single set-cover problem. In this case, the additional benefits that geometric information provides are compromised by the inaccuracy of the greedy solution. An advantage of the multiview-linking

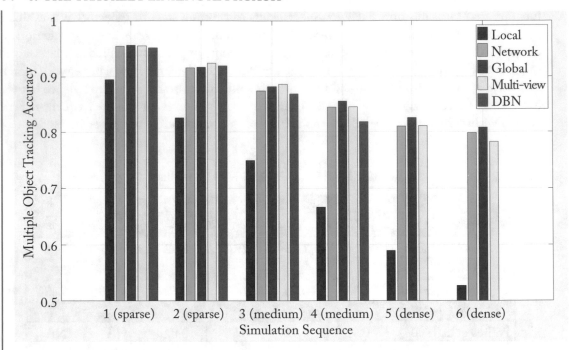

Figure 6.2: Comparison of the MOTA score on a simulation dataset with increasing density. The MOTA score is averaged over all test sequences for each density category. The methods compared here are local linking, network linking, global linking, multiview linking, and the dynamic Bayesian network method proposed by Nillius et al. [2006].

method is that, as a byproduct, it gives the trajectory correspondences between views, which can be seen as a track-to-track fusion and can be used further for 3D path reconstruction (see Chapter 5).

CHAPTER 7

Advanced Techniques for Data Association

In this chapter, we introduce several advanced data association techniques that are either extensions, built on top of classic approaches, or representative novel ideas that just emerged recently. These techniques present unique challenges in the computer vision domain and inspire new research directions for multi-object visual tracking.

7.1 DATA ASSOCIATION FOR MERGED OR SPLIT MEASUREMENTS

Traditional data association methods typically are designed with the assumptions that each measurement can only be uniquely assigned to a track, and a track only produces at most one measurement at each time step. However, "merged" or "split measurements" are actually common in image data, as shown in Fig. 7.1. Multi-object tracking approaches that use complicated measurement models to accommodate such scenarios allow multiple trackers to share a single measurement, and assume that a tracker can produce more than one measurement.

An extension to the Global Nearest Neighbor Standard Filter to handle merged and split measurements was proposed by Kirubarajan et al. [2001] and applied to tracking cells in microscopy time-lapse image sequences. Here, the measurements are the pixel regions of segmented cells. Adjacent cells may be connected due to inaccurate image segmentation, and a cell may be broken into several disconnected components. The standard 2D assignment formulation was extended to assignments in multiple iterations. The algorithm solves a one-to-one assignment at each iteration and produces four sets: a set of tracks, $\mathcal{T}_1$, that receive real measurements; a set of tracks, $\mathcal{T}^0$, that do not have real measurements assigned; a set of measurements, $\mathcal{M}_1$, that originate from the real tracks; and a set of measurements, $\mathcal{M}_0$, that are declared to be false alarms. Then two additional 2D assignment problems are created between $\mathcal{T}_1$ and $\mathcal{M}_0$, $\mathcal{T}_0$ and $\mathcal{M}_1$, respectively. The association cost is augmented to take into account the level of iterations, i.e., it becomes more and more difficult to assign real measurements to real tracks as the iteration level increases. Basically, the iterative process gives tracks and measurements more chances to be paired, which has the effect of enabling one-to-many/many-to-one mappings.

A similar idea was applied to the across-view association scenario by Wu et al. [2009a], where the measurements are image projections of flying animals observed with multiple thermal

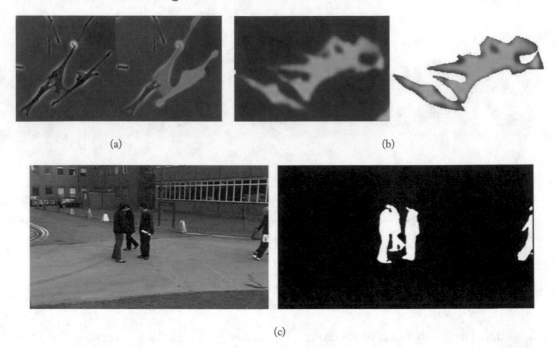

(a)   (b)

(c)

Figure 7.1: Examples of merged and split measurements. (a) An image of a three interacting cells observed with time-lapse phase-contrast microscopy (left) [Wu et al., 2012]. After an appropriate foreground-background segmentation step is performed, a single merged segmented region that corresponds to the three cells is produced (right). (b) Flying animals in infrared video, which occlude each other (left) [Wu et al., 2014]. After a background subtraction step, a merged binary region is produced from the overlapping image projections of multiple animals. (c) Pedestrian tracking in video from the PETS2009 benchmark [Ellis et al., 2009]. A merged binary region, obtained from background subtraction, represents three closely spaced pedestrians.

cameras. Occluded animals generated a single segmented region on image plane, which led to a many-to-one multi-assignment problem. An iterative process was developed based on the standard one-to-one GRASP solver introduced in Sec. 5.3. Merged measurements had more chances to be associated with different animals with an increasing cost.

The main problem with the iterative multi-level assignment approach described above is that the user has to make an ad-hoc design decision to augment the association cost with the algorithm iteration level. The number of times a measurement or track can be assigned is then implicitly controlled by the iteration level. It would be better to work with an estimate on how many objects are present in a merged measurement or how many fragments could be generated from a single object. This is possible in some scenarios where object interactions can be predicted. For tracking cells in microscopy, for example, a merged contour of a known number of interactive cells can be accurately segmented into individual cells through partial boundary matching [Wu et al., 2012]. For tracking groups of people, a merged "blob" can be segmented at the pixel level so that pixels can be shared among different groups through multiple hypotheses under the probabilistic data association filtering framework [Gennari and Hager, 2004].

Note that one can easily model an optimal many-to-one/one-to-many association as a minimum weighted edge cover problem by relaxing the constraints in the 2D assignment problem in Eq. (2.8) to be inequality constraints. But the cost should not be defined directly as the negative log-likelihood of the measurement, as pointed out by Joo and Chellappa [2007]. For example, when two objects are merged into a single measurement, the sum of the two individual association costs that associate the measurement to each object independently could be unreasonably large due to poor localization after merging. A more appropriate definition of the association cost was proposed by Joo and Chellappa [2007] who used the framework of Multiple Hypothesis Tracking.

Instead of sharing the measurements among different tracks to allow many-to-one/one-to-many matching in the measurement-to-track assignment, virtual measurements can be created to extend the measurement set, so that each track may be associated with exactly one (real or virtual) measurement. This idea was proposed by Genovesio and Olivo-Marin [2004] who inserted the ability to have merging and splitting hypotheses into the traditional probabilistic data association framework. Their method maximizes the probability over the newly created joint association events. The work by Stephan and Grinberg [2012] is similar, but they limit their method to only involve two objects in a merging hypothesis. With carefully designed merging and splitting operations, the augmented measurement set can provide better indications of where the objects are and thus improve the estimates of the state of the track.

The enumeration of the merge and split hypotheses requires a computationally prohibitive effort. As we have seen in Chapter 3, a powerful approximation technique to deal with an exponentially large set of association hypotheses is the Markov chain Monte Carlo (MCMC) sampling approach. Two representative MCMC-based algorithms have been proposed to handle the complex measurement model for online and batch processing, respectively [Khan et al., 2006, Yu et al., 2007]. The online algorithm developed by Khan et al. [2006] is a Bayesian recursive filter that estimates the posterior of the joint object states given the history of all measurements. The measurement-to-track association hypothesis is here modeled as a bipartite graph. The merged measurement likelihood is conditioned on one or multiple object states and represented by one or more edges in the bipartite graph connecting the measurement to multiple objects. It is important to use a joint measurement likelihood model here, as opposed to an independent likelihood model used by classic approaches. The joint likelihood model enables the application of a more realistic generative process. For example, the predicted centroid of the merged measurement is the average of the predicted centroid of all objects involved in the merging events. The full evaluation of the posterior is intractable due to the large space of the bipartite graph, so Khan et al. [2006] apply sequential Monte Carlo approximation using the particle filter framework.

Alternatively, the batch algorithm by Yu et al. [2007] is an extension to the MCM-CDA approach explained in Chapter 3, which Yu et al. [2007] named "Spatiotemporal Monte Carlo Markov Chain Data Association." Two new types of MCMC moves were designed—segmentation and aggregation moves. A segmentation move can be proposed when there is sufficiently large overlap between an observed measurement and the predicted measurements from several tracks, which implies a possible merge event. An aggregation move can be proposed when a predicted measurement from a track has sufficiently large overlap with more than one observed measurement, which implies the measurement might split into several disconnected regions. Through a proper parameter training step, this enhanced MCMC-based batch approach can converge reasonably quickly in practice.

Finally, data association with merged and split measurements for long-period tracking can also be implemented with a track-linking approach, using a graph inference procedure. We demonstrated such an example in Sec. 6.2. More examples can be found in the works by Bose et al. [2007], Ma et al. [2006], Perera et al. [2006], and Wu et al. [2011b]. Another interesting problem is the scenario where objects themselves, not the measurements, can merge or split. Such an example was discussed by Makris and Prieur [2014], who used a modified Multiple Hypothesis Tracking scheme for tracking clouds in infrared satellite images.

7.2   LEARNING-BASED DATA ASSOCIATION

Data association can be **learned** from training data. The motivation to incorporate machine learning techniques here is that it is not so straightforward to design a proper distance/similarity measure that evaluates how likely a measurement-to-track assignment is true. When simple motion dynamics are used as features (location, velocity), a Gaussian noise model is usually adopted for computational convenience. However, the Gaussian assumption might not hold when complex features are used, including higher-order motion dynamics (linear or nonlinear), object appearance (color, intensity, intensity gradient, etc.), and related meta data generated from the sensor (time stamps). It is impractical to fine-tune these features manually in order to produce a robust similarity cost function, hoping that it generalizes across datasets. Instead, identifying discriminant features and learning a meaningful metric from training data is a more promising approach. The idea of learning-based data association has been explored by Bae and Yoon [2014], Kim et al. [2012], Kuo et al. [2010a,b], Leal-Taixe et al. [2016], Li et al. [2009], Manen et al. [2016], Sankaranarayanan and Davis [2011], and Xiang et al. [2015].

As shown in Fig. 7.2, a typical learning-based data association approach consists of several steps in a pipeline. A key step is to generate reliable training examples. Positive examples are the right associations of the measurements from the same object. They can be collected offline from ground-truth training data, or online from tracks that are deemed accurate with high confidence. Negative examples are the false associations made when objects are occluding each other or are closely spaced. Negative examples also include the associations between true detections and false alarms.

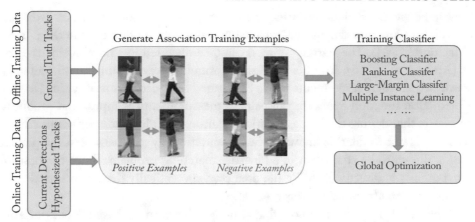

Figure 7.2: A general workflow for learning-based data association. Typically, a training example is a pair of measurements (or their feature representations). Training examples can be generated either offline with the ground truth data, or online with the established track history. A prediction function is learned from the training set that takes a new pair of measurements and decides if they should be associated or not. If the prediction is given for a single pair, then a global optimization step is necessary to find the best associations between all pairs.

Once the set of training examples is constructed, the goal is to learn a discriminative prediction function that takes a pair (or pairs) of measurements and produces a decision on whether they could be associated or not. The decision can be a binary decision or a real-valued score to reflect the decision confidence. The actual learning procedure depends on the choice of the prediction function. Since many predictors only operate on a single pair of measurements, a final global optimization step has to be constructed to solve the data association between two sets of measurements. One advantage of the learning-based approach is that the prediction function is flexible to take arbitrary types of features that are not limited to simple motion dynamics (locations and velocities). This also implies the learning-based approach can be applied to an asynchronized system or multi-model sensor fusion, as long as the training examples are properly defined.

In the work of Li et al. [2009], a hybrid ranking and classification function was learned through boosting, where the final strong predictor is a weighted combination of weak predictors. The ranking part ranks the correct association hypotheses higher than the false ones, while the classification part rejects association hypotheses that are not needed. For example, if an object is not visible in the current frame, there is no association for that object. The prediction confidence score is used as a modified similarity measure and placed in the bipartite matching framework to compute the complete data association solution.

An extension has been developed for the online learning scenario [Kuo et al., 2010b]. Another idea is to substitute the global optimization step with a Conditional Random Field (CRF) model [Yang and Nevatia, 2012]. The CRF model is adopted in order to capture the pairwise relationship between associations during an interactive process, such as objects crossing each other. The prediction function can also be implemented as a max-margin classifier, e.g., a Support Vector Machine (SVM). The learning process can be embedded in a reinforcement learning framework [Xiang et al., 2015]. Another interesting formulation is to jointly predict all the associations between two sets of measurements with a Structured Support Vector Machine [Kim et al., 2012]. The prediction function here takes all pairs of measurements as inputs and produces an assignment matrix that defines the best association solution. Training a learner with a structured output (the output is not a scalar) is known to be computationally expensive, but the prediction step in testing is shown to be equivalent to a bipartite matching problem. Since the best joint association hypothesis is directly given by the predictor, theoretically there is no need to add a global optimization step afterward for this method.

Finally, it is important to note that although the learning-based data association approach is appealing, there are challenges that require further study. On one hand, reliable training sets and labels from ground truth tracks are not always available, especially for those informative examples (or so-called hard examples) that can maximize the performance of the learner. A data mining strategy could be designed to identify the informative training examples that help resolve ambiguous association cases. On the other hand, collecting training examples from online established tracks as the tracking algorithm progresses is more flexible, and it bypasses the issue of having the labeled training data as a prerequisite. But a single, falsely labeled data point can pollute the overall learning accuracy and start to introduce model drifting, a notorious problem inherent in almost all online learning applications.

7.3   COUPLING DATA ASSOCIATION

Traditionally, a data association method is applied to solve an isolated subproblem in a multi-object tracking system: It takes the output of an object detector as its input and produces the estimated trajectories as its output. We call this type of classic architecture a "detection-tracking framework." Under this system architecture, most previous efforts explored two distinct directions of research for improving multi-object tracking: building stronger object detectors and designing better data association methods. In fact, as we have explained in Chapter 4, the common protocol for evaluating a tracking method uses a fixed set of detections to test only the data association part of the method.

The detection-tracking framework has the inherent weakness that it requires the output of the detection step to be reliable in order for the data association step to work properly. Detection errors such as "false alarms" and "missed detections" otherwise propagate to the data association step and false matches need to be corrected later. Intuitively, one can expect that the error propagation from detection to data association can be avoided if both tasks are combined into a single joint inference problem and solved simultaneously. Moreover, solving the data association task can also be helpful to provide feedback to the object detector by providing prior information about image regions where the detector response might be weak. Therefore, a joint inference formulation, which takes advantage of the often complementary nature of the two subproblems, is more promising for handling difficult tracking scenarios. We call this new system architecture "coupled detection and data association."

One can even go further and jointly solve other tasks together with the data association through a single objective function. For example, a segmentation subproblem may refer to the task of labeling the foreground superpixels for each individual object so that partial occlusion can be resolved properly even if the detector fails. A clustering subproblem may refer to the task of identifying groups of objects moving together so that tracking accuracy can be improved using grouping knowledge. In this section, we briefly introduce four representative algorithms falling into this category [Leibe et al., 2008, Milan et al., 2015, Qin and Shelton, 2015, Wu and Betke, 2016].

Formulating the Coupling of Object Detection and Trajectory Estimation as a Model Selection Problem. One of the early coupling ideas for pedestrian tracking was proposed by Leibe et al. [2008], who coupled object detection and data association through a quadratic Boolean function. The intuition of this method is that when an "overcomplete set" [Lewicki and Sejnowski, 2000] of hypothetical trajectories is generated only a small subset is needed to best explain all the image evidence. Searching for such a subset can be formulated as an optimization procedure for model selection according to the Minimum Length Description (MDL) criterion. Here, the savings in coding length of a hypothetical model h, in a high-level description, are expressed as

$$S_h \approx S_{data} - k_1 S_{model} - k_2 S_{error}, \tag{7.1}$$

where S_{data} is the size of data points explained by the model h, S_{model} is the cost of coding the model itself that penalizes a complex model, and S_{error} describes the cost of the error when the data is not perfectly fitted to the model, e.g., the log-likelihood of assigning the data to the model h. The ideal solution for model selection, according to the Minimum Description Length (MDL) criterion, is to use a minimum set of models to explain all the input data points at the expense of low model complexity and data fitting error. Readers may refer to the early work by Leonardisa and Bischof [1998] for discussion of MDL-based machine learning applications. In the context of multi-object tracking, this means the minimum number of trajectories constructed from a series of detections.

To formulate *model selection* as an optimization problem, one has to define the cost for each putative detection and trajectory. Because each data point is assumed to be assigned to one model only (one-to-one matching), overlapping multiple models may compete for the data points. This competition leads to pairwise interaction costs between models. Once all the costs are properly defined, the proposed objective function takes the form of a Quadratic Boolean Problem (QBP):

$$\max_{\mathbf{m},\mathbf{v},\mathbf{n}} \left[\mathbf{m}^T \mathbf{v}^T \mathbf{n}^T \right] \begin{bmatrix} \tilde{Q} & U & V \\ U^T & R & W \\ V^T & W^T & \tilde{S} \end{bmatrix} \begin{bmatrix} \mathbf{m} \\ \mathbf{v} \\ \mathbf{n} \end{bmatrix}, \tag{7.2}$$

where the following definitions apply:

- Indicator vector **n** is used to select detection hypotheses to explain image evidence from a set of putative detections.

- Indicator vector **m** is used to select trajectory hypotheses from a pool of overcomplete hypothetical trajectories formed from detections in the 3D space-time volume.

- Indicator vector **v** is used select "virtual trajectories," one for each detection, so that detections can be used to explain the event of a new object arrival.

- Matrix $\tilde{Q}$ contains individual costs as the diagonal elements for each putative trajectory, i.e., a data association hypothesis, and the pairwise interaction costs as the off-diagonal elements when two trajectories overlap in the space-time volume.

- Matrix $\tilde{S}$ contains individual costs for each putative detection, and the pairwise interaction costs that arise when two detections occupy the same pixel.

- Diagonal matrix R assigns a constant cost ϵ to its diagonal elements to encode the prior knowledge of a detection being generated from a new object in the scene.

- The elements of matrices V and W model the interactions between putative detections and hypothetical trajectories. A detection can contribute to a compatible real trajectory through the entry in V and a virtual trajectory through W.

- Matrix U models the mutual exclusion between the two groups, e.g., a detection already assigned to a real trajectory should not be assigned to a virtual trajectory.

An iterative EM-like procedure can be developed to solve Eq. (7.2). The procedure optimizes detection selector **n** and **v** while fixing the trajectory selector **m** from the past frame, then updates the trajectory selector **m** given the estimated **n** and **v**. Each subproblem can be shown to be submodular so that a multibranch ascent method [Schindler et al., 2006] can be applied to find strong local maxima. Implementation details of the method can be found in the work by Leibe et al. [2008]. In this work, the overcomplete set of detection and trajectory hypotheses was generated incrementally in the online setting. To control the problem size under the limited computing resources, hypothesis initialization and necessary pruning become crucial for a successful application of this method in practice.

Coupling Object Detection and Data Association as a MAP Estimation Problem. The second coupling framework developed by Wu and Betke [2016] is designed for a batch process. The coupled objective function is based on maximizing the posterior probability using Bayesian estimation theory. Compared to the previous coupling work, this method does not need to generate the overcomplete set of hypotheses, which would be impractical for a batch process due to the exponentially growing number of hypotheses. Instead, as we will see, the interaction between the two tasks is controlled by Lagrangian multipliers that dynamically alter the behavior of detection and data association algorithms until an agreement is achieved between the two. The only requirement for this method is that both the object detector and data association algorithm need to be expressed by an optimization formulation.

To derive the coupling objective function as a maximum-*a-posteriori* estimation problem, given a collection $\mathbf{Y}$ of image evidence, we estimate the state of all objects $\mathbf{X}$ in the scene as follows:

$$
\begin{aligned}
&\max_{\mathbf{X}} p(\mathbf{X}|\mathbf{Y}) \\
\propto\ &\max_{\mathbf{X}} p(\mathbf{Y}|\mathbf{X})\,p(\mathbf{X}) \\
=\ &\max_{\mathbf{X}} \prod_t p(\mathbf{Y}_t|\mathbf{X}_t)\,p(\mathbf{X}_1) \prod_t p(\mathbf{X}_t|\mathbf{X}_{t-1}),
\end{aligned}
\tag{7.3}
$$

where $p(\mathbf{Y}_t|\mathbf{X}_t)$ is the image likelihood conditioned on all objects, and the joint state of all objects is governed by a Markov process. After taking the negative logarithm of Eq. (7.3), we rewrite the optimization problem as follows:

$$
\min_{\mathbf{X}_1,\mathbf{X}_2} g(\mathbf{X}_1,\mathbf{Y}) + h(\mathbf{X}_2), \quad s.\,t.\ \mathbf{X}_1 = q(\mathbf{X}_2),
\tag{7.4}
$$

where $\mathbf{X}_1$ and $\mathbf{X}_2$ are two copies of the hidden state variables, g is the function that models the detection problem, h the function that models the data association problem and q the function that enforces the agreement between the solutions $\mathbf{X}_1$ and $\mathbf{X}_2$ of the two subproblems. More specifically, $g(\mathbf{X}_1,\mathbf{Y})$ is minimized to estimate the states $\mathbf{X}_1$ of objects from image evidence $\mathbf{Y}$ and $h(\mathbf{X}_2)$ is minimized to infer the states $\mathbf{X}_2$ of objects from motion or other types of prior knowledge. Naively, q is the identity function that forces $\mathbf{X}_1 = \mathbf{X}_2$.

In the work by Wu and Betke [2016], function g is instantiated as a sparse signal recovery problem to explain the foreground binary pixels with a minimum set of binary shape templates from a pre-defined dictionary. The function h, which handles data association, is defined as a minimum-cost network flow function (Sec. 3.2). As a result, the coupling objective function is

$$
\begin{aligned}
\min_{\mathbf{X}_t, f, t=1,\ldots,T} \quad & \sum_t \|Y_t - \mathbf{D}\mathbf{X}_t\|_1 + \sum_{t,i,j} c_{i,j}^{(t)} f_{i,j}^{(t)} \\
\text{s. t.} \quad & \sum_i f_{i,n}^{(t)} = \sum_j f_{n,j}^{(t)}, \quad \forall t, \forall n \\
& x_{t,n}^{(t)} = \sum_j f_{n,j}^{(t)}, \quad \forall t, \forall n \\
& \mathbf{f} \geq 0, \ \text{and} \ \mathbf{X}_t \in \{0,1\}^N,
\end{aligned}
\tag{7.5}
$$

where the entries of the selection variable $\mathbf{X}_t$ indicate the presence of an object at a particular location at time t. The linear combination of the selected columns in the dictionary matrix D

approximates the observed foreground pixels Y_t. The flow variable $\mathbf{f}$ is used in the minimum-cost flow problem, where $f_{i,j} = 1$ means there is a match between detections at locations i and j, which belong to the same track. The first set of constraints with flow variables ensures a balance of flow. The second set of constraints with flow and selection variables ensures *consistency* between the two local variables $\mathbf{X}$ and $\mathbf{f}$. In other words, if there is a true detection at location n at time t, i.e, $x_{t,n} = 1$, there must be a flow going through the same location at the same time, i.e, $f_{n,j}^{(t)} = 1$ for some j.

The objective function above can be decomposed into two kinds of subproblems, each of which can be solved with an efficient off-the-shelf algorithm. It ensures the coordination of separate minimizers until an agreement is achieved. This approach can be pursued by formulating the Lagrangian dual problem to the original minimization problem (constraints are omitted) [Wu and Betke, 2016]:

$$L(\lambda) \quad = \quad \min_{\mathbf{X},\mathbf{f}} \sum_t \|Y_t - DX_t\|_1 + \lambda_t^T X_t + \sum_{t,i,j}(c_{i,j}^{(t)} - \lambda_{t,i}) f_{i,j}^{(t)}. \tag{7.6}$$

Here λ_t is a vector of the Lagrangian multipliers associated with the coupling constraints $x_{t,n} = f_{n,j}^{(t)}$ defined in Eq. (7.5). According to the dual decomposition technique [Bertsekas, 1999], the so-called master problem can be separated into $(T + 1)$ independent subproblems as follows, where T is the number of frames:

$$g_t(\lambda) \quad = \quad \min_{\mathbf{X}_t}[\|Y_t - DX_t\|_1 + \lambda_t^T X_t]$$
$$h(\lambda) \quad = \quad \min_{\mathbf{f}} \sum_{t,i,j}(c_{i,j}^{(t)} - \lambda_{t,i}) f_{i,j}^{(t)}.$$

Now the dual problem is to maximize $\sum_t g_t(\lambda) + h(\lambda)$ with variable λ, which can be solved by a subgradient method.

The Lagrange multiplier λ will be updated based on the discrepancy between $\mathbf{X}$ and $\mathbf{f}$ in each iteration. It can be seen as a weighting parameter to bias the behavior of the detector or the network flow. For the detection subproblem, a higher value of λ implies a lower preference for detection at a particular location. For the data association subproblem, a higher value of λ leads to a lower edge cost, so it attracts flows passing through that edge. When agreement is achieved, the optimal global solution is obtained for the primal objective function. The detection output is guaranteed to be smooth because of the influence of data association. The flow computation produces tracks as the final output. By changing the value of λ dynamically through dual decomposition, false alarms can be suppressed and detections missed can be recovered. A diagram of this iterative process along with other components in the proposed tracking system is shown in Fig. 7.3.

Since the coupling algorithm is an iterative process, one can expect to see a dynamic change of the quality of the output tracks, which converges to the optimal solution asymptotically. Typically, the overall tracking performance, measured by the MOTA score (Chapter 4), increases

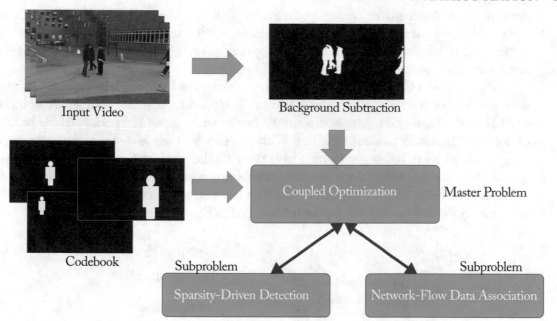

Figure 7.3: Overview of the coupled optimization in a MAP framework for multi-object tracking. The image evidence is the processed foreground/background estimation after background subtraction. The codebook of the scene encodes the shape appearance prior at different scene locations. The coupling objective function is to select codewords (associated with object locations) from the codebook to best explain the foreground pixels, and these codewords should form mutually exclusive trajectories. To optimize this coupling function, the dual decomposition method creates two subproblems and solves them independently first, then checks if the solutions agree with each other.

quickly during the first few iterations, and the amount of disagreement between the two sets of variables, $\mathbf{X}$ and $\mathbf{f}$, decreases drastically. A detailed performance report on standard benchmarks can be found in the work by Wu and Betke [2016].

Coupling Object Segmentation and Data Association as a CRF Inference Problem. The third coupling example of this chapter is the work by Milan et al. [2015]. It goes beyond the previous two methods, which only couple data association with object detection, and also addresses segmentation.

Usually an object detector is designed to only return a restricted set of non-maximum suppressed measurements. When an object appears partially in an image sequence, due to lack of pixel support, the detector may consistently fail even if it is placed in a coupling framework. However, low-level image pixel evidence is still available, and it should not be discarded even though the detector fails. In order to track objects that only partially appear in an image sequence, the fine-grained association between (super-)pixels and objects should be considered. This motivates a coupling framework that integrates (super-)pixel-to-object association, detection-to-object association, and trajectory estimation. In the work by Milan et al. [2015] such an integration is casted as a multi-label conditional random field (CRF) problem.

To see how a CRF model for multi-object tracking can be constructed, we first assume an overcomplete set of trajectory hypotheses is given. This provides an initial label set $\mathcal{L}$ that includes track IDs or background clutter labels. Let $\mathcal{V}_S$ be the set of superpixel nodes and $\mathcal{V}_D$ be the set of detection nodes. A random variable v is associated with each node from the node set $\mathcal{V} = \mathcal{V}_S \bigcup \mathcal{V}_D$, which can be assigned with a label from $\mathcal{L}$. The edge set $\mathcal{E} = \mathcal{E}_S \bigcup \mathcal{E}_T \bigcup \mathcal{E}_D$ models spatial and temporal connections between neighboring superpixels, as well as the relationship between superpixels and the detection bounding box that surrounds them. An example of the CRF model for two consecutive frames is illustrated in Fig. 7.4.

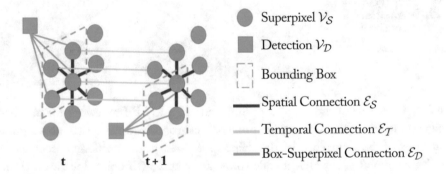

Figure 7.4: Example of a Conditional Random Field for joint segmentation and tracking in two frames. The trajectory hypothesis assigns labels to each detection as well as each superpixel. A detection generated by some object detector is a bounding box that may occupy multiple superpixels, which is represented by edges in $\mathcal{E}_D$. The spatial and temporal neighboring relationships between superpixels are represented by red and blue edges in $\mathcal{E}_S$ and $\mathcal{E}_T$, respectively.

The ideal labeling v^* for all nodes given the image evidence is the minimizer of a global energy E as follows:

$$v^* = \arg\min_v E(\mathcal{V}) = \arg\min_v \left(\sum_{s \in \mathcal{V}_S} \phi^{\mathcal{V}_S}(s) + \sum_{d \in \mathcal{V}_D} \phi^{\mathcal{V}_D}(d) + \sum_{(v,w) \in \mathcal{E}} \psi(v,w) + \psi^\lambda \right), \quad (7.7)$$

where $\phi^{\mathcal{V}_S}$ and $\phi^{\mathcal{V}_D}$ are the unary potentials for superpixels and detections, respectively, that measure the compatibility between measurements and trajectory hypotheses, and where $\psi(v,w)$ is the pairwise potential that enforces consistent labelings between neighboring nodes, both spatially and temporally. The prior cost ψ^λ of each trajectory hypothesis encourages a smoothed trajectory in terms of object appearance and dynamics. Details of the implementation of each potential term is described in the paper by Milan et al. [2015]. The key in designing the objective function E is to make it submodular so that the inference is tractable.

Note that the output of the CRF inference does not only solve the data association problem (trajectories) but also produces segmentations for all objects at the superpixel level. The spirit of this method is similar to the first coupling example by Leibe et al. [2008], because it also aims to search for an optimal subset of trajectory hypotheses from an overcomplete set. But the method has to deal with the data association at a lower granularity. Although it has been shown that low-level features such as superpixels and motion flows can improve tracking performance [Chen et al., 2014, Fragkiadaki et al., 2012], this method is more suitable for an offline batch process due to the significantly increased computation burden.

Coupling Data Association and Group Clustering through Social Group Model The last example in this chapter follows a recent trend to model crowd behavior from videos, where multi-object tracking serves as a basic module to produce trajectories for further analysis. The topic of crowd modeling and behavior analysis is beyond the scope of this book [Dehghan et al., 2013, Yamaguchi et al., 2011], but it is worth mentioning that properly modeling social groups and their behavior in the scene is also beneficial to improve multi-object tracking accuracy. For example, the motion model, commonly designed as a constant-velocity model, was enhanced by Pellegrini et al. [2009]. This approach takes into account scene information and social interactions between objects. The performance of the traditional tracklet stitching method and the traditional network-flow data association method was also improved by encoding social behavior information in their similarity measures [Leal-Taixé et al., 2014, 2011, Zhang et al., 2013].

Several methods have been proposed to jointly solve data association and social behavior modeling. The method by Choi and Savarese [2012] jointly models the tracklet stitching process through network flow and the activity recognition for each person as well as the group. The collective activities provide social contextual cues for making data association more robust; in turn, the estimated trajectories enable construction of more accurate interaction and collective activity models. In [Pellegrini et al., 2010], data associations and group memberships are jointly estimated through a high-order CRF model. The model, though expressive, is computationally expensive for inference. A more efficient solution was proposed by Qin and Shelton [2015], who coupled the same subproblems in a constrained nonlinear optimization framework. In the following, we give a brief outline of this method.

The input to the method by Qin and Shelton [2015] is a set of tracklets, $\tau = \{\tau_1, \tau_2, ..., \tau_n\}$. The data association task is to determine which tracklets correspond to the same object. The solution to this task can be represented as a binary assignment matrix ϕ, i.e., $\phi_{i,j} = 1$ only if tracklet τ_j immediately follows τ_i. To ensure a tracklet can only follow one or be followed by one other tracklet, we can add linear constraints that $\sum_j \phi_{i,j} = 1$ and $\sum_i \phi_{i,j} = 1$. The social grouping task is to determine the number K of groups and the membership of each tracklet. Each group contains one or multiple tracklets, and a group mean trajectory G_k. Let $G = \{G_1, G_2, ..., G_K\}$

and the membership be represented as a binary grouping matrix ψ, i.e., $\psi_{i,k} = 1$ if tracklet i is assigned to group k. Again, a valid grouping matrix requires a constraint that $\sum_k \psi_{i,k} = 1$. Denote the space of valid assignment and grouping matrices to be Φ and Ψ, respectively. By jointly solving two subproblems in a single objective function, one can show that a MAP formulation for a given number K of groups leads to the following nonlinear constrained optimization problem:

$$\min_{\phi \in \Phi, \psi \in \Psi, G} \quad \sum_{i,j} \phi_{i,j} H_{i,j} + \sum_{i,k} \psi_{i,k} D(\tau_i, G_k)$$

$$s.t. \quad \phi_{i,j}(\psi_{i,k} - \psi_{j,k}) = 0. \ \forall i, j, k, \tag{7.8}$$

where $H_{i,j}$ measures the cost to associate tracklets i and j, and $D_{i,j}$ measures how close tracklet i is from its group mean G_k. Note that the objective function is coupled through the constraint that involves both variables ϕ and ψ, which ensures linked tracklets must be in the same social group. The Lagrangian of Eq. (7.8), with multipliers $\mu_{i,j,k}$, is:

$$L(\phi, \psi, G, \mu) = \sum_{i,j} \phi_{i,j} H_{i,j} + \sum_{i,k} \psi_{i,k} D(\tau_i, G_k) + \sum_{i,j,k} \mu_{i,j,k} \ \phi_{i,j}(\psi_{i,k} - \psi_{j,k}). \tag{7.9}$$

To solve Eq. (7.8), Qin and Shelton [2015] proposed an iterative two-stage alternative optimization scheme. Similar to the dual decomposition technique used in the second coupling example earlier [Wu and Betke, 2016], one can show that the subgradient of the dual of Eq. (7.9) with respect to $\mu_{i,j,k}$ is $\phi_{i,j}^{(\mu)}(\psi_{i,k}^{(\mu)} - \psi_{j,k}^{(\mu)})$, which can be computed in a two-stage block coordinate descend step.

Given the current estimates of μ, the new data association result ϕ is computed first when the grouping variables ψ and G are fixed:

$$\phi^{(\mu)} = \arg\min_{\phi \in \Phi} \sum_{i,j} \phi_{i,j} [H_{i,j} + \sum_k \mu_{i,j,k}(\psi_{i,k} - \psi_{j,k})]. \tag{7.10}$$

Next, the new grouping result (ψ, G) is computed with ϕ fixed:

$$(\psi^{(\mu)}, G^{(\mu)}) = \arg\min_{\psi \in \Psi, G} \sum_{i,k} \psi_{i,k} [D(\tau_i, G_k) + \sum_j (\mu_{i,j,k} \phi_{i,j} - \mu_{j,i,k} \phi_{j,i})]. \tag{7.11}$$

Equation (7.10) can be solved using off-the-shelf algorithms introduced in Chapter 2, and Eq. (7.11) can be solved using the standard K-means clustering algorithm.

To conclude this chapter, we would like to point out that addressing the multi-object tracking problem as a joint estimation problem that captures multiple correlated subproblems is advantageous from a modeling point of view. However, it also brings new challenges to the optimization step. For a small or medium-sized tracking problem, offering a better model has been proven to be useful, even though this approach introduces additional computation costs. Very often, the computational bottleneck is actually in setting up the problem. For a large-sized tracking problem, the benefits need to be balanced between the model accuracy and the computing resource expense. It is also important to note that an algorithm that uses a decomposition technique is more likely to be scalable with the use of a distributed computing system.

CHAPTER 8

Application to Animal Group Tracking in 3D

Various species of animals have been tracked in 2D and 3D by computer vision systems, including bats [Wu, 2012], birds [Attanasi et al., 2015, Evangelista et al., 2015], fish [Giordano et al., 2016, Lee et al., 2010], and insects [Feldman et al., 2012, Veeraraghavan et al., 2008]. In this chapter, we first describe two systems used for 3D tracking of multiple animals in flight and then give examples of the use of such systems to facilitate research in the natural sciences. Both systems require solving data association across time and across view, and they rely on techniques introduced in previous chapters.

8.1   TWO SAMPLE SYSTEMS FOR ANALYZING BAT AND BIRD FLIGHT

To date, two systems exist that have been used to reconstruct the 3D flight paths of thousands of animals, one system was developed at Boston University, the other at the University of Rome. The number of 3D flight paths they have computed is orders of magnitude larger than what has been produced for any previous animal study, and data association is a critical component of each system.

The Boston University EcoTracker. The development of the Boston University EcoTracker goes back to the thesis work by Hirsh [2004], and it was first made available to the research community as a two-dimensional tracking system in 2007 [Bagchi, 2006, Betke et al., 2007, 2008, Immermann et al., 2007] (see Fig. 8.1).

Subsequent versions of EcoTracker, described by Hristov et al. [2008], Premerlani [2007], Towne et al. [2012], Wu et al. [2009a,b, 2011b], and Wu and Betke [2016], improved on the 2D tracking and incorporated reconstruction of 3D flight paths, and 3D tracking. The method by Wu et al. [2009b] is described in Chapter 5, and the methods by Wu et al. [2009a] and Wu and Betke [2016] in Chapter 7.

The work by Theriault et al. [2014], a research team from Boston University and University of North Carolina, then produced a version of EcoTracker that uses the 3D tracking and data association method by Wu et al. [2009a] and includes libraries for camera calibration and simulation code for experiment preparation, in particular, camera placement and error analysis.

Figure 8.1: Sample frames computed by the Boston University EcoTracker. A column of Brazilian free-tailed bats is tracked as the animals fly out of their cave roost. An owl, a predator of bats, is approaching the column from the vegetation (orange flight path). This 2D version of EcoTracker uses the Multi Hypotheses Tracking with gating (see Chapter 2).

Theriault et al. [2014] illustrated the use of their system in two field experiments. They recorded video of Brazilian free-tailed bats at a distance of about 10 m with three synchronized thermal infrared cameras with frame size 1,024 × 1,024 pixels, frame rate of 131.5 Hz, and 14-bit thermal values per pixel. A baseline between the outermost cameras of 6 m was used. For recording video of Cliff Swallows at a distance of about 20 m, they used three synchronized cameras with frame size 2,336 × 1,728, frame rate 100 Hz, and 10-bit brightness values per pixel, and a baseline of 11 m. The root mean squared (RMS) reconstruction uncertainty for 2,796 estimated 3D positions of Cliff Swallows was 5.9 cm, less than half the length of a bird. The RMS reconstruction uncertainty for the 1,656 estimated 3D positions of the bats was 7.8 cm, less than the average length of Brazilian free-tailed bat, which is 10 cm.

The University of Rome STARFLAG/GReTA system. The system by researchers at the University of Rome started out as a multi-camera system, called STARFLAG, to reconstruct the positions of birds in their natural environment in 3D and did not include any tracking [Cavagna et al., 2008b]. It was developed to study the European starlings (*Sturnus vulgaris*) that gather in large flocks within the city of Rome before dusk in the winter months [Cavagna et al., 2008a].

Initial work focused on the camera setup in the field; for example, a baseline of 25 m between cameras was used. With a distance of 100 m between cameras and animals, the length of a bird mapped to 5–15 pixels in the images. Cavagna et al. [2008b] discussed the difficulties of geometrically calibrating the cameras and balancing aperture, light sensitivity, and shutter speed to enhance sharpness and contrast. The 3D positions of flocks of 400–4,000 birds were reconstructed with the STARFLAG system [Cavagna et al., 2008a].

More recently, a tracking algorithm called "GReTA" was added to the STARFLAG system [Attanasi et al., 2015]. It is an off-line algorithm that globally optimizes the data association of tracklets. Such an approach addresses a problem that is equivalent to the joint set cover problem, as had been noted by Wu et al. [2011b]. The GReTA algorithm was tested on simulated 3D trajectories of flocking birds using a model proposed by Bialek et al. [2012] and on experimental field data of starling flocks [Attanasi et al., 2014a], swarms of midges [Attanasi et al., 2014b], and groups of flying bats [Wu et al., 2014].

8.2   IMPACT OF MULTI-ANIMAL TRACKING SYSTEMS

The multi-object tracking systems discussed in this book can facilitate important research results in the natural sciences when they are applied to analyze videos of flying animals. We here briefly highlight the impact in three areas of research.

Facilitating Research in Ecology and Conservation Biology. Counting the number of flight paths of animals is important for censusing natural populations of bats and birds [Betke et al., 2008, 2004, Hristov et al., 2010, 2006, 2007, Kunz et al., 2008]. A census of a population yields a better understanding of the impact these animals can have on ecosystems. Brazilian free-tailed bats (*Tadarida brasiliensis*), for example, eat moths whose larvae destroy corn and cotton crops, so censusing has to be used to estimate the monetary value that the species provides for pest control services [Cleveland et al., 2006].

Analyzing video data collected with a three-camera thermal infrared imaging system, Betke et al. [2008] obtained a 4-million census from six major colonies of Brazilian free-tailed bats (*Tadarida brasiliensis*). With information about additional colonies, the authors projected that 9 million individual bats comprised the total mid-summer cave population of the Brazilian free-tailed bat in the southwestern United States in the mid 2000s, about ten years ago. This is only 6% of the population that was estimated to include 150 million bats in 1957, about 60 years ago.

Filming bats emerging at Carlsbad Caverns during 20 evenings in the summer of 2005, Hristov et al. [2010] found a fluctuation of colony size of as many as 291,000 individuals from one night to the next. The censuses were orders of magnitude lower than the largest historic estimates. Bats appeared in the thermal videos for 20–30 frames, and the computer vision system tracked them for at least 10–15 frames. Emergence rates ranged from 10 to 10,000 bats/minute.

Since hundreds of thousands of flight tracks were reconstructed in the work by Betke et al. [2008], Hristov et al. [2010], it was infeasible to conduct an exhaustive ground-truth comparison. In both works, automated tracking performance and animal counts were validated by human visual inspection of sample results. On average, computed censuses were within 3.7% [Hristov et al., 2010] or even 0.8% [Betke et al., 2008] of the average human observer counts, which were based on thousands of annotations of the same videos. Another way to validate 2D trajectory counts is to compare the results obtained from different camera view points (Fig. 8.2).

Facilitating Research on Animal Flight. Small groups of birds and bats have been tracked simultaneously with computer vision methods to study locomotion and navigation of social animals. Tandem flight behavior has been analyzed for cliff swallows (*Petraochelidon pyrrhonota*) [Shelton et al., 2014] and cave myotis (*Myotis velifer*) [Baillieul et al., 2016, Kong et al., 2014]. Cliff swallows pair flight exhibits a wide range of instantaneous speed and duration. The flight path and wingbeat frequency of the leading bird is copied by the following bird while the following bird flew slightly above the leading bird. For cave myotis, it was found that classical leader-follower motion strategies do not apply, such as "pursuit," i.e., alignment of the direction of motion, and "motion camouflage," i.e., fixing the relative positions of leader and follower [Kong et al., 2014].

Kong et al. [2013] and Baillieul et al. [2016] studied how cave myotis use sensory perception of the environment to control their flight. They proposed control laws for modeling motion trajectories that exhibited characteristics of bat flight. Based on the analysis of 10,000 reconstructed trajectories and audio data of 114 single bats, Baillieul et al. [2016] suggested that bats use vision, passive hearing, echolocation, and spatial memory to navigate in their natural environments.

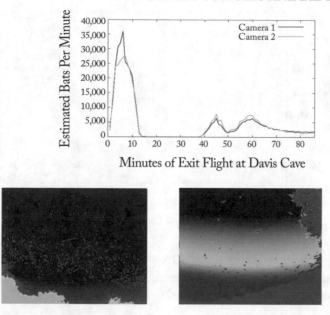

Figure 8.2: Validation experiment: Results of automated tracking of the exit flight of a bat colony observed with thermal infrared cameras from two significantly different viewpoints. The number of tracked bats was 457,422 in the first view and 441,757 in the second, a difference of about 3.4%.

Facilitating Research on Collective Motion. Aggregations of animals, their motion and group behavior, have been investigated since the 19th century [Breder, 1954, Hamilton, 1971, Pryer, 1884] and continue to be actively studied [Attanasi et al., 2014a, Bialek et al., 2012, Bode et al., 2011, Buhl et al., 2006, Calovi et al., 2014, Gerum et al., 2013, Krause et al., 2009, Mann et al., 2013, Nagy et al., 2010, Portugal et al., 2014]. In recent years, as it has become technically feasible to collect large datasets of thousands of observations of animals, detailed studies have been carried out examining the behavior of locusts [Buhl et al., 2006], starlings [Attanasi et al., 2014a, Ballerini et al., 2008a, Bialek et al., 2012, Cavagna et al., 2010], chimney swifts [Evangelista et al., 2015], and Brazilian free-tailed bats [Theriault, 2015].

The more recent data-driven studies of collective motion have provided an opportunity to reexamine existing motion models. Animals have mostly been modeled to move with a constant [Vicsek and Zafeiris, 2012] or random [Aoki, 1982, Huth and Wissel, 1992] speed because early authors [Aoki, 1982] deemed the heading of animals to be the most important aspect of individual motion and assumed that speed changes in response to neighbors could be disregarded or modeled independently. Exceptions include the works by Bode et al. [2010], Mishra et al. [2012], Reif and Wang [1999], Reynolds [1987], Theriault [2015].

Theriault [2015] found that an explicit heading alignment rule is not necessary for ordered motion to arise. Translation, rotation, or milling of the group can emerge spontaneously in Flock-

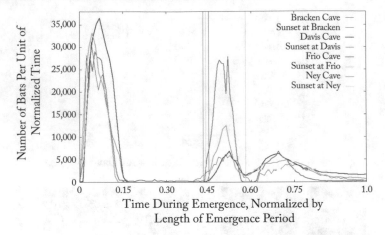

Figure 8.3: Analysis of flight trajectory data for large groups of bats emerging from their caves. A similar pattern is revealed when the time axis is normalized by the four durations of emergence, respectively. The strongest flow of bats happened during episodes before sunset.

Opt, an optimization-based, variable-speed, self-propelled model of collective motion. The model also predicts that individual variations in speed and heading serve to maintain relative positions between group members. This is consistent with the analysis of thousands of 3D trajectories of bats in flight that were obtained using multi-object tracking.

We conclude this chapter by giving an example of a phenomenon of collective motion that was discovered when large numbers of reconstructed bat flight trajectories were compared [Betke et al., 2008]. By analyzing the exit flight of colonies of Brazilian free-tailed bats from four different caves, Betke et al. [2008] found that the flow of bats during their exiting periods had a unique multi-episodal pattern that was independent of the size of the bat colony. In triple-episode emergences, the occurrence of peaks seem to have a characteristic rhythm, independent of the tempo of the emergence. The phenomenon was measured by comparing the number of emerging bats per unit of time for each cave colony against a time axis that was normalized by the respective durations of the emergence of the full colony (Fig. 8.3). The description of this phenomenon triggered research on emergence cohorts, which found that lactating bats emerge earlier than pregnant bats, and juveniles emerged later than adult females [Reichard et al., 2009].

CHAPTER 9

Benchmarks for Human Tracking

Despite the steady progress in the algorithmic development for multi-object tracking, there has been very limited work on standardizing quantitative evaluation. Performance was used to be reported on small, unreleased datasets, and it was very difficult to assess a new algorithm or give any empirical study of state-of-the-art techniques. Recently, some datasets have been extensively used in the community, such as CAVIAR [List et al., 2005],[1] ETH [Ess et al., 2007],[2] EPFL [Fleuret et al., 2008],[3] TUD [Andriluka et al., 2010],[4] PETS-2009 [Ellis et al., 2009],[5] AVG [Benfold and Reid, 2009],[6] Trecvid [Yang et al., 2011],[7] UCF-PNNL [Dehghan et al., 2015],[8] BU-TIV [Wu et al., 2014],[9] and KITTI [Geiger et al., 2012].[10] Almost all of them are human tracking datasets, but differ in camera setup (moving or static), sensor modality (visible light or infrared), image resolution, and crowd density. Among these datasets, PETS-2009 is probably the most widely used benchmark, primarily for surveillance applications. An overview of the datasets that allow open access is given in Table 9.1.

9.1 PETS-2009

The PETS-2009 dataset [Ellis et al., 2009] contains three subsets of data—each was designed for a different task:

S1: people counting and density estimation,

S2: people tracking,

S3: crowd flow analysis and event recognition.

Subsets S1–S3 all contain multiple sequences. The subset most relevant to the material in our book is S2, and so we here discuss the performance of state-of-the art methods on this subset:

---

[1]http://groups.inf.ed.ac.uk/vision/CAVIAR/CAVIARDATA1
[2]http://www.vision.ee.ethz.ch/~aess/dataset
[3]http://cvlab.epfl.ch/data/pom
[4]http://www.d2.mpi-inf.mpg.de/datasets
[5]http://www.cvg.rdg.ac.uk/PETS2009
[6]http://www.robots.ox.ac.uk/ActiveVision/Research/Projects/2009bbenfold_headpose/project.html
[7]http://www-nlpir.nist.gov/projects/tv2008
[8]http://crcv.ucf.edu/data/ParkingLOT
[9]http://csr.bu.edu/BU-TIV/BUTIV.html
[10]http://www.cvlibs.net/datasets/kitti

Table 9.1: An overview of publicly available data sets for multi-object tracking

Dataset Name	Publications	Frames	Views	Density	Camera
CAVIAR	List et al., 2005	37,224	2	low	static
EPFL	Fleuret et al., 2008	22,890	3–4	low	static
PETS-2009	Ellis et al., 2009	2,371	1–8	low, medium, high	static
TUD	Andriluka et al., 2010	451	1	medium	static
ETH	Ess et al., 2007	4,047	1	medium	moving
AVG	Benfold and Reid, 2009	4,500	1	medium	static
UCF	Dehghan et al., 2015	2,661	1	medium, high	static
KITTI-MOT	Geiger et al., 2012	19,103	1–2	medium	moving
BUTIV-MOT	Wu et al., 2014	19,458	1–3	low, medium	static
MOTChallenge	Leal-Taixé et al., 2015a	11,286	1	low, medium, high	static, moving

S2L1: This is the easiest sequence for people tracking. In a given frame, it only shows approximately five pedestrians per frame. Most state-of-the-art methods can achieve accuracies of over 90% on S2L1, and so for this sequence, trying to improve performance any further may not make sense as it may lead to overfitting.

S2L2: In this sequence, pedestrians occur with "medium density" of approximately 20 pedestrians per frame (see Fig. 9.1).

S2L3: In this sequence, pedestrians occur with "high density" of approximately 40 pedestrians per frame (see Fig. 9.1).

Figure 9.1: Sample images from PETS-2009 benchmark.

The sequences S2L2 and S2L3 present many challenging scenarios, including frequent mutual interactions and partial or complete occlusions. As a result, designers of more recent algorithms started to test on these more difficult sequences [Milan et al., 2014, Possegger et al., 2014, Wu et al., 2013].

Despite the popularity of the PETS 2009 dataset in the community, there are several concerns on the proper usage of the dataset. First, the originally stated instructions for the use of the dataset, as formulated at the PETS 2009 Workshop, did not require users to test their algorithms on all the sequences in this benchmark. So many published methods were never tested on the complete benchmark. When results on a few of the sequences with higher density were shown, it was not clear how representative these results were and whether unintentional "cherry picking" occurred.

Second, the PETS team does not release the ground-truth annotations. It holds a workshop approximately once a year to which researchers are invited to submit their results for an evaluation by the team. Outside this annual event, reported tracking results are often inconsistent. In addition to selective use of sequences, independent ground-truth labeling efforts have been made, and a variation of detection inputs and evaluation protocols have been utilized.

Third, the PETS 2009 dataset is limited in its scope. All the sequences show the same scene. The camera positions were fixed, and the background is relatively stable with little lighting changes. The dataset does not contain sequences with large background changes that, for example, would occur with the use of moving cameras.

The aforementioned concerns motivate the need for a more diversified benchmark for multi-object tracking, as well as a standardization of evaluation protocols, as will be discussed next.

9.2   BEYOND PETS-2009: THE MOT-CHALLENGE BENCHMARK

To overcome the limitation of PETS benchmark, and to generalize the data so that they are sufficiently variable and difficult to overfit, a new benchmark, MOTChallenge [Leal-Taixé et al., 2015a,b],[11] was released to the public in 2015 (see Fig. 9.2). This benchmark assembled several sequences from the existing datasets, including ETH [Ess et al., 2007], TUD [Andriluka et al., 2010], PETS-2009 [Ellis et al., 2009], AVG [Benfold and Reid, 2009], and KITTI [Geiger et al., 2012]. Sequences were separated into the training and testing sets to have a balanced distribution, and the ground-truth data was only given for the training set. The diversification can be viewed in three perspectives:

a) The cameras were placed on a moving platform or were fixed in the scene.

b) The viewpoint was set at positions of different heights. The viewpoint at a lower position typically introduces heavy occlusions.

---

[11]https://motchallenge.net

c) The sequences were captured under different lighting conditions, resulting in sunny, cloudy and night scenes.

Figure 9.2: Sample images from MOTChallenge benchmark.

Additionally, detection results from the ACF detector [Dollár et al., 2014], along with results from a few of baseline methods, are provided. CLEAR MOT and USC metrics were adopted for quantitative evaluation. Baseline methods achieve about 20% MOTA score[12] on average (see Table 9.2). More recent methods have approached a 50% MOTA score, which shows that there is room for much improvement of tracking algorithms.

Table 9.2: Performance of baseline algorithms on MOTChallange benchmark

Method Name	MOTA	Description
JPDA Rezatofighi et al., 2015	23.8 ± 15.1	Joint Probabilistic Data Association (Sec. 2.4)
MHT Kim et al., 2015	32.4 ± 15.6	Multiple Hypothesis Tracking (Sec. 2.5)
Network Flow Pirsiavash et al., 2011	14.5 ± 13.9	Min-cost Network Flow Association (Sec. 3.2)
Energy Minimization Milan et al., 2014	19.3 ± 17.5	A continuous but non-convex minimization formulation

---

[12]Results from MOTChallenge website were accessed on March, 2016.

The organizers plan to expand this centralized MOTChallenge benchmark on a yearly basis [Milan et al., 2016], and we foresee that the MOTChallenge benchmark will definitely push research in tracking toward more generic and robust solutions.

CHAPTER 10

Concluding Remarks

Data association for multi-object tracking is a fundamental problem in computer vision with broad impact on many practical applications. Research on data association has progressed rapidly in the last thirty years. Classic methods, as described in Chapters 2 and 3, were first developed for radar applications and then revisited in the computer vision domain during the last ten years. Unlike the point measurements in radar scans, the measurements in computer vision involve extended image regions with far more complicated objects that require more sophisticated tracking algorithms (see Chapters 5–7). Reports about algorithm performance on standard benchmarks (Chapter 9) suggest that there is still much room for improvement of the current state-of-the-art algorithms. Recent trends focus on the following two aspects of data association.

On one hand, researchers try to design better features to ease the difficulty of computing correct associations. Efforts include introducing machine learning to identify discriminant features, building descriptors for tracklets, or integrating both low-level and mid-level features. A good feature typically plays an important role in many computer vision tasks. If the unique "signature" of each object can be identified via its features, data association across time or across view is simply a re-identification task. Recent success in deep learning for computer vision will encourage research in this direction—deeply learned object features may provide signatures that facilitate data association.

On the other hand, many recent works construct a "global" optimization framework that models some or all factors that may influence the motion of objects. These factors include mutual occlusions, scene structure, camera topology, social group, etc. Such an optimization framework, by its nature, is fairly complex, and usually one can only expect to achieve a sub-optimal solution through some level of approximation. Interestingly, an exact global optimum has never been the focus of research along this line. The key value lies in the model itself, as well as its generalization to broader tracking scenarios.

Additionally, an urgent need for an objective evaluation protocol (Chapter 4) and better benchmarks (Chapter 9) has emerged, without which new algorithms are difficult to assess, even for experts in this field. An even more pressing concern is that very few implementations of the new algorithms are open to the public. This fact can be frustrating for researchers, given that many published papers do not explain all the details, and the methods are becoming more and more complicated. We therefore encourage researchers to share their implementations and thereby benefit the whole community.

Finally, we also expect to see a wider range of applications beyond surveillance or autonomous driving. People and vehicles will remain the central objects of interest, but multi-object tracking and data association are also critical to make other scientific studies possible. In this book, we use the study of large groups of flying animals as an example (Chapter 8). Multi-object tracking problems exist in biomedical/medical sciences, material science, astronomy, etc. Obviously, there is a great opportunity for researchers in this field to extend their findings and facilitate scientific discoveries. This is particularly true nowadays, as big data becomes ubiquitous.

Bibliography

Ahuja, R. K., Magnanti, T. L. and Orlin, J. B. (1993). *Network Flows: Theory, Algorithms, and Applications*. Prentice-Hall, Inc. 24

Ali, S. and Shah, M. (2008). Floor fields for tracking in high density crowd scenes. In *Proc. of the 10th European Conference on Computer Vision (ECCV)*, pp. 1–14. DOI: 10.1007/978-3-540-88688-4_1. 2

Andrade, E., Blunsden, S. and Fisher, R. (2006). Performance analysis of event detection models in crowded scenes. In *Proc. of the Workshop "Towards Robust Visual Surveillance Techniques and Systems" at Visual Information Engineering 2006*, pp. 427–432. Bangalore, India. DOI: 10.1049/cp:20060569. 2

Andriluka, M., Roth, S. and Schiele, B. (2008). People-tracking-by-detection and people-detection-by-tracking. In *Proc. the IEEE Conference on Computer Vision and Pattern Recognition (CVPR)*, pp. 1–8. DOI: 10.1109/cvpr.2008.4587583. 47

Andriluka, M., Roth, S. and Schiele, B. (2010). Monocular 3d pose estimation and tracking by detection. In *Proc. of the IEEE Computer Society Conference on Computer Vision and Pattern Recognition*. DOI: 10.1109/cvpr.2010.5540156. 77, 79

Andriyenko, A. and Schindler, K. (2010). Globally optimal multi-target tracking on a hexagonal lattice. In *Proc. of the European Conference on Computer Vision*, pp. 1–8. DOI: 10.1007/978-3-642-15549-9_34. 25

Aoki, I. (1982). A simulation study on the schooling mechanism in fish. *Bulletin of the Japanese Society of Scientific Fisheries*, 48. DOI: 10.2331/suisan.48.1081. 75

Attanasi, A., Cavagna, A., Castello, L. D., Giardina, I., Jelic, A., Melillo, S., Parisi, L., Pellacini, F., Shen, E., Silvestri, E. and Viale, M. (2015). GReTA—A novel global and recursive tracking algorithm in three dimensions. *IEEE Transactions on Pattern Analysis and Machine Intelligence*, 37, pp. 2451–2463. DOI: 10.1109/tpami.2015.2414427. 46, 71, 73

Attanasi, A., Cavagna, A., Del Castello, L., Giardina, I., Grigera, T. S., Jelic, A., Melillo, S., Parisi, L., Pohl, O., Shen, E. and Viale, M. (2014a). Information transfer and behavioural inertia in starling flocks. *Nature Physics*, 10, pp. 691–696. DOI: 10.1038/nphys3035. 73, 75

Attanasi, A., Cavagna, A., Del Castello, L., Giardina, I., Parisi, L., Pohl, O., Rossaro, B., Shen, E., E., S. and M., V. (2014b). Collective behaviour without collective order in wild swarms of midges. *PLoS Computational Biology*, 10, e1003697. DOI: 10.1371/journal.pcbi.1003697. 3, 73

Bae, S.-H. and Yoon, K.-J. (2014). Robust online multi-object tracking based on tracklet confidence and online discriminative appearance learning. In *Proc. of the IEEE Conference on Computer Vision and Pattern Recognition (CVPR)*, pp. 1218–1225. DOI: 10.1109/cvpr.2014.159. 58

Bagchi, A. (2006). A clustered data association technique for expedited multi target tracking. Master's thesis, Boston University. 71

Baillieul, J., Kong, Z., Fuller, N., Wang, S., Özcimder, K., Gillam, E., Theriault, D. and Betke, M. (2016). Perceptual modalities guiding bat flight in a native habitat. *Scientific Reports*. DOI: 10.1038/srep27252. 74

Bak, S., Chau, D. P., Badie, J., Corvee, E., Bremond, F. and Thonnat, M. (2012). Multi-target tracking by discriminative analysis on Riemanian manifold. In *Proc. of the 19th International Conference on Image Processing (ICIP)*. DOI: 10.1109/icip.2012.6467182. 47

Ballerini, M., Cabibbo, N., Candelier, R., Cavagna, A., Cisbani, E., Giardina, I., Lecomte, V., Orlandi, A., Parisi, G., Procaccini, A., Viale, M. and Zdravkovic, V. (2008a). Interaction ruling animal collective behavior depends on topological rather than metric distance: Evidence from a field study. In *Proc. of the National Academy of Sciences*, 105, pp. 1232–1237. DOI: 10.1073/pnas.0711437105. 75

Ballerini, M., Cabibbo, N., Candelier, R., Cavagna, A., Cisbani, E., Giardina, I., Orlandi, A., Parisi, G., Procaccini, A., Viale, M. and Zdravkovic, V. (2008b). Empirical investigation of starling flocks: a benchmark study in collective animal behaviour. *Animal Behaviour*, 76, pp. 201–215. DOI: 10.1016/j.anbehav.2008.02.004. 3

Bar-Shalom, Y. and Fortmann, T. E. (1988). *Tracking and Data Association*. Academic Press. DOI: 10.1121/1.398863. 7, 12

Bar-Shalom, Y. and Li, X. R. (1995). *Multitarget—Multisensor Tracking: Principles and Techniques*. YBS Publishing. 11, 13, 16, 46

Bar-Shalom, Y. X., Li, R. and Kirubarajan, T. (2001). *Estimation with Applications to Tracking and Navigation*. John Wiley & Sons, Inc. DOI: 10.1002/0471221279. 8

Benfold, B. and Reid, I. (2009). Guiding visual surveillance by tracking human attention. In *Proc. of the British Machine Vision Conference*. DOI: 10.5244/c.23.14. 77, 79

Benfold, B. and Reid, I. (2011). Stable multi-target tracking in real-time surveillance video. In *Proc. of IEEE Conference on Computer Vision and Pattern Recognition (CVPR)*, pp. 3457–3464. DOI: 10.1109/cvpr.2011.5995667. 21

Berclaz, J., Fleuret, F. and Fua, P. (2009). Multiple object tracking using flow linear programming. In *Proc. of the IEEE Workshop on Performance Evaluation of Tracking and Surveillance (PETS)*. DOI: 10.1109/pets-winter.2009.5399488. 25

Berclaz, J., Fleuret, F., Tretken, E. and Fua, P. (2011). Multiple object tracking using k-shortest paths optimization. *IEEE Transactions on Pattern Analysis and Machine Intelligence*, 33, pp. 1806–1819. DOI: 10.1109/tpami.2011.21. 25

Bernardin, K. and Stiefelhagen, R. (2008). Evaluating multiple object tracking performance: The CLEAR MOT metrics. *EURASIP Journal on Image and Video Processing*. 2008. DOI: 10.1155/2008/246309. 29

Bertsekas, D. P. (1991). *Linear Network Optimization: Algorithms and Codes*. MIT Press. 11

Bertsekas, D. P. (1999). *Nonlinear Programming*. Belmont, MA: Athena Scientific. DOI: 10.1038/sj.jors.2600425. 64

Bertsekas, D. P. and Castañón, D. A. (1992). A forward/reverse auction algorithm for asymmetric assignment problems. *Computational Optimization and Applications*, 1, pp. 277–297. DOI: 10.1007/bf00249638. 11

Betke, M., Haritaoglu, E. and Davis, L. S. (2000). Real-time multiple vehicle detection and tracking from a moving vehicle. *Machine Vision and Applications*, 12, pp. 69–83. http://www.cs.bu.edu/fac/betke/papers/betke-mva00.pdf. DOI: 10.1007/s001380050126. 3

Betke, M., Hirsh, D. E., Bagchi, A., Hristov, N. I., Makris, N. C. and Kunz, T. H. (2007). Tracking large variable numbers of objects in clutter. In *Proc. of the IEEE Computer Society Conference on Computer Vision and Pattern Recognition (CVPR)*, p. 8. Minneapolis, MN. http://www.cs.bu.edu/fac/betke/papers/Betke-etal-cvpr07.pdf. DOI: 10.1109/cvpr.2007.382994. 71

Betke, M., Hirsh, D. E., Makris, N. C., McCracken, G. F., Procopio, M., Hristov, N. I., Tang, S., Bagchi, A., Reichard, J. D., Horn, J. W., Crampton, S., Cleveland, C. J. and Kunz, T. H. (2008). Thermal imaging reveals significantly smaller Brazilian free-tailed bat colonies than previously estimated. *Journal of Mammalogy*, 89, pp. 18–24. http://www.asmjournals.or g/doi/pdf/10.1644/07-MAMM-A-011.1pdf. Also discussed in *Nature*, 452, Research Highlights, p. 507, http://www.cs.bu.edu/fac/betke/papers/nature-embattled-bats-Ap ril2008.pdf. DOI: 10.1644/07-mamm-a-011.1. 2, 3, 71, 73, 74, 76

Betke, M., Kunz, T. H., Tang, S. and Hirsh, D. E. (2004). Censusing Brazilian free-tailed bats with infrared thermal imaging—challenges, lessons learned, and initial results. In *Proc. of the 34th Annual North American Symposium on Bat Research (NASBR)*, p. 26. Salt Lake City, UT. http://www.cs.bu.edu/fac/betke/papers/Betke-et-al-NASBR-2004.pdf. 73

Betke, M., Ruel, J., Sharp, G. C., Jiang, S. B., Gierga, D. P. and Chen, G. T. Y. (2006). Tracking and prediction of tumor movement in the abdomen. In *Pattern Recognition in Information Systems: Proceedings of the 6th International Workshop on Pattern Recogntion in Information Systems—PRIS 2006* (eds. A. Fred and A. Lourenço), pp. 27–37. Paphos, Cyprus: INSTICC Press. http://www.cs.bu.edu/fac/betke/papers/BetkeRuelSharpJiangGiergaChen-2006.pdf. 3

Bialek, W., Cavagna, A., Giardina, I., Mora, T., Silvestri, E., Viale, M. and Walczak, A. M. (2012). Statistical mechanics for natural flocks of birds. *Proc. of the National Academy of Sciences*, 109, pp. 4786–4791. DOI: 10.1073/pnas.1118633109. 73, 75

Bise, R., Li, K., Eom, S. and Kanade, T. (2009). Reliably tracking partially overlapping neural stem cells in dic microscopy image sequences. In *MICCAI Workshop on Optical Tissue Image Analysis in Microscopy, Histopathology and Endoscopy (OPTMHisE)*. 3

Bise, R., Yin, Z. and Kanade, T. (2011). Reliable cell tracking by global data association. In *Proc. of IEEE International Symposium on Biomedical Imaging (ISBI)*, pp. 1004–1010. DOI: 10.1109/isbi.2011.5872571. 48

Bishop, C. M. (2007). *Pattern Recognition and Machine Learning*. Springer. 19

Black, J., Ellis, T. and Rosin, P. (2003). A novel method for video tracking performance evaluation. In *PETS*, pp. 125–132. 29

Blackman, S. (2004). Multiple hypothesis tracking for multiple target tracking. *IEEE Aerospace and Electronic Systems Magazine*, 19, pp. 5–18. DOI: 10.1109/maes.2004.1263228. 17

Blackman, S., Dempster, R. and Reed, R. (2001). Demonstration of multiple hypothesis tracking (MHT) practical real-time implementation feasibility. In *Proc. of SPIE Signal and Data Processing of Small Targets*, pp. 470–475. DOI: 10.1117/12.492756. 17

Blackman, S. and Popoli, R. (1999). *Design and Analysis of Modern Tracking Systems*. Artech House, Boston, London. 8, 9

Bode, N. W. F., Faria, J. J., Franks, D. W., Krause, J. and Wood, A. J. (2010). How perceived threat increases synchronization in collectively moving animal groups. *Proc. of the Royal Society B: Biological Sciences*, 277, pp. 3065–3070. DOI: 10.1098/rspb.2010.0855. 75

Bode, N. W. F., Franks, D. W. and Wood, A. J. (2011). Limited interactions in flocks: relating model simulations to empirical data. *Journal of The Royal Society Interface*, 8, pp. 301–304. DOI: 10.1098/rsif.2010.0397. 75

Bose, B., Wang, X. and Grimson, E. (2007). Multi-class object tracking algorithm that handles fragmentation and grouping. In *Proc. of the IEEE Conference on Computer Vision and Pattern Recognition (CVPR)*, pp. 1–8. DOI: 10.1109/cvpr.2007.383175. 50, 58

Breder, C. M. (1954). Equations descriptive of fish schools and other animal aggregations. *Ecology*, 35, pp. 361–370. DOI: 10.2307/1930099. 75

Brostow, G. J. and Cipolla, R. (2006). Unsupervised Bayesian detection of independent motion in crowds. In *Proc. of the IEEE Conference on Computer Vision and Pattern Recognition (CVPR)*, pp. 594–601. DOI: 10.1109/cvpr.2006.320. 2

Brown, R. G. and Hwang, P. Y. C. (1997). *Introduction to Random Signals and Applied Kalman Filtering*. John Wiley & Sons, Inc. 7, 11

Buhl, J., Sumpter, D. J. T., Couzin, I. D., Hale, J. J., Despland, E., Miller, E. R. and Simpson, S. J. (2006). From disorder to order in marching locusts. *Science*, 312, pp. 1402–1406. DOI: 10.1126/science.1125142. 75

Cai, Y. and Medioni, G. (2014). Exploring context information for inter-camera multiple target tracking. In *Proc. of the IEEE Winter Conference on Applications of Computer Vision (WACV)*, pp. 1–8. DOI: 10.1109/wacv.2014.6836026. 47

Calovi, D. S., Lopez, U., Ngo, S., Sire, C., Chaté, H. and Theraulaz, G. (2014). Swarming, schooling, milling: phase diagram of a data-driven fish school model. *New Journal of Physics*, 16, 015026. DOI: 10.1088/1367-2630/16/1/015026. 75

Carr, P. and Collins, R. T. (2016). Assessing tracking performance in complex scenarios using mean time between failures. In *Proc. of the IEEE Winter Conference on Applications of Computer Vision (WACV)*, pp. 1–8. DOI: 10.1109/wacv.2016.7477617. 34

Castañón, D. A. (1990). Efficient algorithms for finding the k best paths through a trellis. *IEEE Transactions on Aerospace and Electronic Systems*, 26, pp. 405–410. DOI: 10.1109/7.53448. 23, 24

Castañón, G. and Finn, L. (2011). Multi-target tracklet stitching through network flows. In *Proc. of the IEEE Aerospace Conference, Big Sky, MT*, p. 7. DOI: 10.1109/aero.2011.5747436. 47, 48

Cavagna, A., Cimarelli, A., Giardina, I., Orlandi, A., Parisi, G., Procaccini, A., Santagati, R. and Stefanini, F. (2008a). New statistical tools for analyzing the structure of animal groups. *Mathematical biosciences*, 214, pp. 32–37. DOI: 10.1016/j.mbs.2008.05.006. 73

Cavagna, A., Cimarelli, A., Giardina, I., Parisi, G., Santagati, R., Stefanini, F. and Viale, M. (2010). Scale-free correlations in starling flocks. In *Proc. of the National Academy of Sciences*. DOI: 10.1073/pnas.1005766107. 75

Cavagna, A., Giardina, I., Orlandi, A., Parisi, G., Procaccini, A., Viale, M. and Zdravkovic, V. (2008b). The STARFLAG handbook on collective animal behaviour: 1. Empirical methods. *Animal Behaviour*, 76, pp. 217–236. DOI: 10.1016/j.anbehav.2008.02.002. 73

Chan, A. B. and Vasconcelos, N. (2012). Counting people with low-level features and Bayesian regression. *IEEE Transactions on Image Processing*, 21, pp. 2160–2177. DOI: 10.1109/tip.2011.2172800. 2

Chari, V., Lacoste-Julien, S., Laptev, I. and Sivic, J. (2015). On pairwise costs for network flow multi-object tracking. In *Proc. of the IEEE Conference on Computer Vision and Pattern Recognition*. DOI: 10.1109/cvpr.2015.7299193. 25

Chen, S., Fern, A. and Todorovic, S. (2014). Multi-object tracking via constrained sequential labeling. In *Proc. of the IEEE Conference on Computer Vision and Pattern Recognition (CVPR)*, pp. 1130–1137. DOI: 10.1109/cvpr.2014.148. 67

Chenouard, N., Bloch, I. and Olivo-Marin, J.-C. (2009). Multiple hypothesis tracking in microscopy images. In *Proc. of IEEE International Symposium on Biomedical Imaging*, pp. 1346–1349. Boston. DOI: 10.1109/isbi.2009.5193314. 15

Choi, W. and Savarese, S. (2012). A unified framework for multi-target tracking and collective activity recognition. In *Proc. of the 12th European Conference on Computer Vision (ECCV)*, pp. 215–230. DOI: 10.1007/978-3-642-33765-9_16. 67

Cleveland, C. J., Betke, M., Federico, P., Frank, J. D., Hallam, T. G., Horn, J., Jr., J. D. L., McCracken, G. F., Medellín, R. A., Moreno-Valdez, A., Sansone, C. G., Westbrook, J. K. and Kunz, T. H. (2006). Economic value of the pest control service provided by Brazilian free-tailed bats in south-central Texas. *Frontiers in Ecology and the Environment*, 4, pp. 238–248. http://www.cs.bu.edu/fac/betke/papers/Cleveland-et-al-2006.pdfpdf. DOI: 10.1890/1540-9295(2006)004[0238:evotpc]2.0.co;2. 74

Cormen, T. H., Leiserson, C. E. and Rivest, R. L. (1990). *Introduction to Algorithms*. MIT Press/McGraw-Hill. 50

Cox, I. J. and Hingorani, S. L. (1996). An efficient implementation of Reid's multiple hypothesis tracking algorithm and its evaluation for the purpose of visual tracking. *IEEE Transactions on Pattern Analysis and Machine Intelligence*, 18, pp. 138–150. DOI: 10.1109/34.481539. 7, 15, 16

Crouse, D. F., Guerriero, M. and Willett, P. (2009). A critical look at the PMHT. *Journal of Advances in Information Fusion*, 4, pp. 93–116. 27

Deb, S., Yeddanapudi, M., Pattipati, K. and Bar-Shalom, Y. (1997). A generalized s-d assignment algorithm for multisensor-multitarget state estimation. *IEEE Transaction on Aerospace and Electronic Systems*, 33, pp. 523–538. DOI: 10.1109/7.575891. 17, 18, 44

Dehghan, A., Assari, S. M. and Shah, M. (2015). Gmmcp-tracker:globally optimal generalized maximum multi clique problem for multiple object tracking. In *Proc. of IEEE Computer Vision and Pattern Recognition*. DOI: 10.1109/cvpr.2015.7299036. 18, 77

Dehghan, A., Idrees, H., Zamir, A. R. and Shah, M. (2013). Automatic detection and tracking of pedestrians in videos with various crowd densities. In *Pedestrian and Evacuation Dynamics 2012*, pp. 3–19. DOI: 10.1007/978-3-319-02447-9_1. 67

Dempster, A. P., Laird, N. M. and Rubin, D. B. (1977). Maximum likelihood from incomplete data via the em algorithm. *Journal of the Royal Statistical Society, Series B*, 39, pp. 1–38. 26

Dicle, C., Sznaier, M. and Camps, O. (2013). The way they move: Tracking targets with similar appearance. In *Proc. of the International Conference on Computer Vision (ICCV)*. DOI: 10.1109/iccv.2013.286. 47, 48

Dockstader, S. L. and Tekalp, A. M. (2001). Multiple camera fusion for multi-object tracking. In *Proc. of the IEEE Workshop on Multi-Object Tracking*. DOI: 10.1109/mot.2001.937987. 38, 40

Dollár, P., Appel, R., Belongie, S. and Perona, P. (2014). Fast feature pyramids for object detection. *IEEE Transactions on Pattern Analysis and Machine Intelligence*, 36, pp. 1532–1545. DOI: 10.1109/tpami.2014.2300479. 80

Doretto, G., Sebastian, T., Tu, P. and Rittscher, J. (2011). Appearance-based person reidentification in camera networks: Problem overview and current approaches. *Journal of Ambient Intelligence and Humanized Computing*, pp. 127–151. DOI: 10.1007/s12652-010-0034-y. 38

Ellis, A., Shahrokni, A. and Ferryman, J. M. (2009). Pets2009 and winter-pets 2009 results: a combined evaluation. In *Proc. of the IEEE Workshop on Performance Evaluation of Tracking and Surveillance (PETS)*. DOI: 10.1109/pets-winter.2009.5399728. 56, 77, 79

Erdem, U. M. and Sclaroff, S. (2012). Event prediction in a hybrid camera network. *ACM Transactions on Sensor Networks (TOSN)*, 8. DOI: 10.1145/2140522.2140529. 38

Eshel, R. and Moses, Y. (2008). Homography based multiple camera detection and tracking of people in a dense crowd. In *Proc. of the IEEE Conference on Computer Vision and Pattern Recognition (CVPR)*. DOI: 10.1109/cvpr.2008.4587539. 38, 39, 40

Ess, A., Leibe, B. and Gool, L. (2007). Depth and appearance for mobile scene analysis. In *Proc. of the IEEE Computer Society Conference on Computer Vision and Pattern Recognition*. DOI: 10.1109/iccv.2007.4409092. 77, 79

Evangelista, D., Khandelwal, P., Rader, J. and Hedrick, T. L. (2015). Free-flight kinematics of massed chimney swifts entering a chimney roost at dusk. In *Society for Integrative and Comparative Biology 2015 Annual Meeting*. 91.3. 3, 71, 75

Feldman, A., Hybinette, M. and Balch, T. (2012). The multi-iterative closest point tracker: An online algorithm for tracking multiple interacting targets. *Journal of Field Robotics*, 29, pp. 258–276. DOI: 10.1002/rob.21402. 71

Fisher, J. L. and Casasent, D. P. (1989). Fast JPDA multi-target tracking algorithm. *Applied Optics*, 28, pp. 371–376. DOI: 10.1364/ao.28.000371. 14

Fitzgerald, R. J. (1985). Track biases and coalescence with probabilistic data association. *IEEE Transactions on Aerospace and Electronic Systems*, 21, pp. 822–825. DOI: 10.1109/taes.1985.310670. 15

Fleuret, F., Berclaz, J., Lengagne, R. and Fua, P. (2008). Multi-camera people tracking with a probabilistic occupancy map. *IEEE Transactions on Pattern Analysis and Machine Intelligence*, 30, pp. 267–282. DOI: 10.1109/tpami.2007.1174. 38, 39, 40, 77

Forsyth, D. A. and Ponce, J. (2003). *Computer Vision: A Modern Approach*. Prentice Hall, NJ. 8

Fragkiadaki, K., Zhang, W., Zhang, G. and Shi, J. (2012). Two-granularity tracking: mediating trajectory and detection graphs for tracking under occlusions. In *Proc. of the 12th European Conference on Computer Vision (ECCV)*, pp. 552–565. DOI: 10.1007/978-3-642-33715-4_40. 67

Gauvrit, H., Le Cadre, J. P. and Jauffret, C. (1997). A formulation of multitarget tracking as an incomplete data problem. *IEEE Transaction on Aerospace and Electronic Systems*, 33, pp. 1242–1257. DOI: 10.1109/7.625121. 26

Ge, W. and Collins, R. T. (2008). Multi-target data association by tracklets with unsupervised parameter estimation. In *Proc. of British Machine Vision Conference (BMVC)*. DOI: 10.5244/c.22.93. 21, 47

Geiger, A., Lenz, P. and Urtasun, R. (2012). Are we ready for autonomous driving? the kitti vision benchmark suite. In *Proc. of the IEEE Computer Society Conference on Computer Vision and Pattern Recognition*. DOI: 10.1109/cvpr.2012.6248074. 77, 79

Gennari, G. and Hager, G. (2004). Probabilistic data association methods in visual tracking of groups. In *Proc. of the IEEE Conference on Computer Vision and Pattern Recognition (CVPR)*, pp. 876–881. DOI: 10.1109/cvpr.2004.1315257. 57

Genovesio, A. and Olivo-Marin, J. C. (2004). Split and merge data association filter for dense multi-target tracking. In *Proc. of the IEEE International Conference on Pattern Recognition (ICPR)*, pp. 677–680. DOI: 10.1109/icpr.2004.1333863. 57

Gerum, R. C., Fabry, B., Metzner, C., Beaulieu, M., Ancel, A. and Zitterbart, D. P. (2013). The origin of traveling waves in an emperor penguin huddle. *New Journal of Physics*, 15, 125022. DOI: 10.1088/1367-2630/15/12/125022. 75

Giordano, D., Palazzo, S. and Spampinato, C. (2016). Chapter 10: Fish tracking. In *Fish4Knowledge: Collecting and Analyzing Massive Coral Reef Fish Video Data*, (ed. R. B. Fisher). Springer International Publishing Switzerland. DOI: 10.1007/978-3-319-30208-9. 71

Habtemariam, B., Tharmarasa, R., Thayaparan, T., Mallick, M. and Kirubarajan, T. (2013). A multiple-detection joint probabilistic data association filter. *IEEE Journal Selected Topics in Signal Processing*, 7, pp. 461–471. DOI: 10.1109/jstsp.2013.2256772. 15

Hamilton, W. D. (1971). Geometry for the selfish herd. *Journal of Theoretical Biology*, 31, pp. 295–311. DOI: 10.1016/0022-5193(71)90189-5. 75

Hartley, R. I. and Zisserman, A. (2003). *Multiview View Geometry in Computer Vision*. Cambridge University Press. DOI: 10.1017/cbo9780511811685. 43, 45

Henriques, J. F., Caseiro, R. and Batista, J. (2011). Globally optimal solution to multi-object tracking with merged measurements. In *Proc. of the International Conference on Computer Vision (ICCV)*, pp. 2470–2477. DOI: 10.1109/iccv.2011.6126532. 47

Herbert-Read, J. E., Perna, A., Mann, R. P., Schaerf, T. M., Sumpter, D. J. T. and Ward, A. J. W. (2011). Inferring the rules of interaction of shoaling fish. In *Proc. of the National Academy of Sciences*, 108, pp. 18726–18731. DOI: 10.1073/pnas.1109355108. 3

Hirsh, D. E. (2004). Evaluation of computer vision methods for analyzing infrared thermal video and censusing Brazilian free-tailed bats, Boston university, bachelors thesis. 71

House, D., Walker, M. L., Wu, Z., Wong, J. Y. and Betke, M. (2009). Tracking of cell populations to understand their spatio-temporal behavior in response to physical stimuli. In *MMBIA 2009: IEEE Computer Society Workshop on Mathematical Methods in Biomedical Image Analysis*, p. 8. Miami, FL. http://www.cs.bu.edu/fac/betke/papers/House-etal-MMBIA-2009.pdf. DOI: 10.1109/cvprw.2009.5204057. 3

Hristov, N. I., Betke, M., Hirsh, D., Bagchi, A. and Kunz, T. H. (2010). Seasonal variation in colony size of Brazilian free-tailed bats at Carlsbad Caverns using thermal imaging. *Journal of Mammalogy*, 91, pp. 183–192. http://www.asmjournals.org/doi/pdf/10.1644/08-MAMM-A-391R.1. DOI: 10.1644/08-mamm-a-391r.1. 73, 74

Hristov, N. I., Betke, M. and Kunz, T. H. (2006). Lessons in history: Colony size and population decline of Brazilian free-tailed bats at Carlsbad Caverns. In *Proc. of the 36th Annual North American Symposium on Bat Research (NASBR)*. Wilmington, NC. 73

Hristov, N. I., Betke, M. and Kunz, T. H. (2007). Lessons in history: Colony size and population decline of Brazilian free-tailed bats at Carlsbad Caverns. In *Society for Integrative and Comparative Biology (SICB), 2007 Annual Meeting*. Phoenix, AZ. http://www.sicb.org/m eetings/2007/schedule/abstractdetails.php3?id=526Abstract. 73

Hristov, N. I., Betke, M. and Kunz, T. H. (2008). Applications of thermal infrared imaging for research in aeroecology. *Integrative and Comparative Biology*, 48, pp. 50–59. http://www. cs.bu.edu/fac/betke/papers/HristovBetkeKunz-IntegrCompBiol-2008.pdf. DOI: 10.1093/icb/icn053. 71

Huang, C., Wu, B. and Nevatia, R. (2008). Robust object tracking by hierarchical association of detection responses. In *Proc. of the 10th European Conference on Computer Vision (ECCV)*, pp. 788–801. DOI: 10.1007/978-3-540-88688-4_58. 47, 48

Huth, A. and Wissel, C. (1992). The simulation of the movement of fish schools. *Journal of Theoretical Biology*, 156, pp. 365–385. DOI: 10.1016/s0022-5193(05)80681-2. 75

Idrees, H., Saleemi, I., Seibert, C. and Shah, M. (2013). Multi-source multi-scale counting in extremely dense crowd images. In *IEEE Conference on Computer Vision and Pattern Recognition*, pp. 2547–2554. DOI: 10.1109/cvpr.2013.329. 2

Immermann, E., Theriault, D. H. and Betke, M. (2007). Boston University EcoTracker. http://www.cs.bu.edu/fac/betke/research/bats. 71

Isard, M. and Blake, A. (1998). Condensation—conditional density propagation for visual tracking. *International Journal of Computer Vision*, 29, pp. 5–28. DOI: 10.1023/A:1008078328650. 7, 11

Jiang, H., Fels, S. and Little, J. J. (2007). A linear programming approach for multiple object tracking. In *Proc. of the IEEE Conference on Computer Vision and Pattern Recognition (CVPR)*, pp. 1–8. DOI: 10.1109/cvpr.2007.383180. 24

Joo, S.-W. and Chellappa, R. (2007). A multiple-hypothesis approach for multiobject visual tracking. *IEEE Transactions on Image Processing*, 16, pp. 2849–2854. DOI: 10.1109/tip.2007.906254. 57

Kang, J., Cohen, I. and Medioni, G. (2005). Persistent objects tracking across multiple non-overlapping cameras. In *Proc. of IEEE Workshop on Motion and Video Computing (WMVC)*. DOI: 10.1109/acvmot.2005.92. 38

Kao, E., Daggett, M. and Hurley, M. (2009). An information theoretic approach for tracker performance evaluation. In *Proc. of the International Conference on Computer Vision (ICCV)*, pp. 1523–1529. DOI: 10.1109/iccv.2009.5459275. 29

Kasturi, R., Goldgof, D., Soundararajan, P., Manohar, V., Garofolo, J., Bowers, R., Boonstra, M., Korzhova, V. and Zhang, J. (2009). Framework for performance evaluation of face, text, and vehicle detection and tracking in video: data, metrics, and protocol. *IEEE Transactions on Pattern Analysis and Machine Intelligence*, 31, pp. 319–336. DOI: 10.1109/tpami.2008.57. 29

Katz, Y., Tunstrø m, K., Ioannou, C. C., Huepe, C. and Couzin, I. D. (2011). Inferring the structure and dynamics of interactions in schooling fish. In *Proc. of the National Academy of Sciences*, 108, pp. 18720–18725. DOI: 10.1073/pnas.1107583108. 3

Kay, S. M. (1993). *Fundamentals of Statistical Processing, Volume I: Estimation Theory*. Prentice Hall. 8

Keck, M. and Davis, J. (2011). Recovery and reasoning about occlusions in 3d using few cameras with applications to 3d tracking. *Journal of International Journal of Computer Vision*, 95, pp. 240–264. DOI: 10.1007/s11263-011-0446-y. 39

Kennedy, H. L. (2008). Controlling track coalescence with scaled joint probabilistic data association. In *Proc. of the International Conference on Radar*, pp. 440–445. DOI: 10.1109/radar.2008.4653963. 15

Khan, S. M. and Shah, M. (2006). A multiview approach to tracking people in crowded scenes using a planar homography constraint. In *Proc. of the European Conference on Computer Vision (ECCV)*, volume 3954, pp. 133–146. DOI: 10.1007/11744085_11. 3, 38, 39, 40

Khan, Z., Balch, T. and Dellaert, F. (2006). MCMC data association and sparse factorization updating for real time multitarget tracking with merged and multiple measurements. *IEEE Transactions on Pattern Analysis and Machine Intelligence*, 28, pp. 1960–1972. DOI: 10.1109/tpami.2006.247. 21, 57

Kim, C., Li, F., Ciptadi, A. and Rehg, J. M. (2015). Multiple hypothesis tracking revisited. In *Proc. of the International Conference on Computer Vision (ICCV)*. DOI: 10.1109/iccv.2015.533. 15

Kim, S., Kwak, S., Feyereisl, J. and Han, B. (2012). Online multi-target tracking by large margin structured learning. In *Proc. of the 11th Asian Conference on Computer Vision (ACCV)*, pp. 98–111. DOI: 10.1007/978-3-642-37431-9_8. 58, 60

Kirubarajan, T., Bar-Shalom, Y. and Pattipati, K. (2001). Multiassignment for tracking a large number of overlapping objects and application to fibroblast cells. *IEEE Transactions on Aerospace and Electronic Systems*, 37, pp. 2–21. DOI: 10.1109/7.913664. 55

Kong, Z., Özcimder, K., Fuller, N., Greco, A., Theriault, D., Wu, Z., Kunz, T., Betke, M. and Baillieul, J. (2013). Optical flow sensing and the inverse perception problem for flying bats. In *The 2013 IEEE Conference on Decision and Control (CDC), Florence, Italy*, p. 8. DOI: 10.1109/cdc.2013.6760112. 74

Kong, Z., Özcimder, K., Fuller, N., Theriault, D., Betke, M. and Baillieul, J. (2014). Perception and steering control in paired bat flight. In *The 19th World Congress of the International Federation of Automatic Control (IFAC), South Africa*, p. 7. DOI: 10.3182/20140824-6-za-1003.01670. 74

Krause, J., Lusseau, D. and James, R. (2009). Animal social networks: an introduction. *Behavioral Ecology and Sociobiology*, 63, pp. 967–973. 10.1007/s00265-009-0747-0. DOI: 10.1007/s00265-009-0747-0. 75

Kristan, M., Matas, J. and et al., A. L. (2015). The visual object tracking vot2015 challenge results. In *The IEEE International Conference on Computer Vision (ICCV) Workshops*, pp. 564–586. DOI: 10.1109/iccvw.2013.20. 35

Kunz, T. H., Chau, J. C., Wu, Z., Hong, L., Reichard, J. D., Betke, M. and Little, T. D. C. (2008). A novel, remote-controlled BatCam for censusing small colonies of bats. In *Proc. of the 38th Annual North American Symposium on Bat Research (NASBR)*. Scranton, PA. http://www.cs.bu.edu/fac/betke/papers/Kunz-etal-NASBR-2008.pdfPoster. 73

Kuo, C.-H., Huang, C. and Nevatia, R. (2010a). Inter-camera association of multi-target tracks by on-line learned appearance affinity models. In *Proc. of the 11th European Conference on Computer Vision (ECCV)*, pp. 383–396. DOI: 10.1007/978-3-642-15549-9_28. 58

Kuo, C.-H., Huang, C. and Nevatia, R. (2010b). Multi-target tracking by on-line learned discriminative appearance models. In *Proc. of the IEEE Conference on Computer Vision and Pattern Recognition (CVPR)*, pp. 685–692. DOI: 10.1109/cvpr.2010.5540148. 58, 59

Leal-Taixe, L., Canton-Ferrer, C. and Schindler, K. (2016). Learning by tracking: Siamese CNN for robust target association. In *CVPR Workshop DeepVision: Deep Learning for Computer Vision, Las Vegas, NV*. 58

Leal-Taixé, L., Fenzi, M., Kuznetsova, A., Rosenhahn, B. and Savarese, S. (2014). Learning an image-based motion context for multiple people tracking. In *Proc. of the IEEE Conference on Computer Vision and Pattern Recognition (CVPR)*, pp. 3542–3549. DOI: 10.1109/cvpr.2014.453. 67

Leal-Taixé, L., Milan, A., Schindler, K., Roth, S. and Reid, I. (2015a). Benchmarking multi-target tracking. In *Proc. of the 1st Workshop on Benchmarking Multi-target Tracking*. 4, 79

Leal-Taixé, L., Milan, A., Schindler, K., Roth, S. and Reid, I. (2015b). MOTChallenge 2015: Towards a benchmark for multi-target tracking. *arXiv:1504.01942 [cs]* ArXiv: 1504.01942. 4, 79

Leal-Taixé, L., Pons-Moll, G. and Rosenhahn, B. (2011). Everybody needs somebody: Modeling social and grouping behavior on a linear programming multiple people tracker. In *Proc. of the IEEE Workshop on Modeling, Simulation and Visual Analysis of Large Crowds*, pp. 120–127. DOI: 10.1109/iccvw.2011.6130233. 67

Lee, J.-H., Wu, M.-Y. and Guo, Z.-C. (2010). A tank fish recognition and tracking system using computer vision techniques. In *2010 3rd IEEE International Conference on Computer Science and Information Technology (ICCSIT)*. DOI: 10.1109/iccsit.2010.5563625. 71

Lee, K. H., Choi, M. G., Hong, Q. and Lee, J. (2007). Group behavior from video: a data-driven approach to crowd simulation. In *Proc. of the 2007 ACM SIGGRAPH/Eurographics symposium on Computer animation*, pp. 109–118. Eurographics Association. 3

Leibe, B., Schindler, K., Cornelis, N. and Gool, L. V. (2008). Coupled object detection and tracking from static cameras and moving vehicles. *IEEE Transactions on Pattern Analysis and Machine Intelligence*, 30, pp. 1683–1698. DOI: 10.1109/tpami.2008.170. 61, 62, 67

Leichter, I. and Krupka, E. (2013). Monotonicity and error type differentiability in performance measures for target detection and tracking in video. *IEEE Transactions on Pattern Analysis and Machine Intelligence*, 35, pp. 2553–2560. DOI: 10.1109/tpami.2013.70. 32

Lempitsky, V. and Zisserman, A. (2010). Learning to count objects in images. In *Proc. Advances in Neural Information Processing Systems (NIPS)*, pp. 1324–1332. 2

Lennart, S., Daniel, S., Marco, G. and Peter, W. (2011). Set JPDA filter for multitarget tracking. *IEEE Transactions on Signal Processing*, 59, pp. 4677–4691. DOI: 10.1109/tsp.2011.2161294. 15

Leonardisa, A. and Bischof, H. (1998). An efficient MDL-based construction of RBF networks. *Neural Networks*, 11, pp. 963–973. DOI: 10.1016/s0893-6080(98)00051-3. 61

Lewicki, M. S. and Sejnowski, T. J. (2000). Learning overcomplete representations. *Neural Computation*, 12, pp. 337–365. DOI: 10.1162/089976600300015826. 61

Li, K., Chen, M. and Kanade, T. (2007). Cell population tracking and lineage construction with spatiotemporal context. In *Medical Image Computing and Computer-Assisted Intervention—MICCAI 2007, 10th International Conference, Brisbane, Australia, October 29–November 2, 2007, Proceedings, Part II, Lecture Notes in Computer Science, Volume 4792/2007* (eds. N. Ayache, S. Ourselin and A. Maeder), pp. 295–302. Springer Berlin/Heidelberg. DOI: 10.1007/978-3-540-75759-7. 3

Li, K., Chen, M., Kanade, T., Miller, E., Weiss, L. and Campbell, P. (2008a). Cell population tracking and lineage construction with spatiotemporal context. *Medical Image Analysis*, 12, pp. 546–566. DOI: 10.1016/j.media.2008.06.001. 48

Li, K., Miller, E. D., Chen, M., Kanade, T., Weiss, L. E. and Campbell, P. G. (2008b). Computer vision tracking of stemness. In *Proc. of the 5th IEEE International Symposium on Biomedical Imaging: From Nano to Macro (ISBI 2008)*, pp. 847–850. DOI: 10.1109/isbi.2008.4541129. 3

Li, K., Miller, E. D., Weiss, L. E., Campbell, P. G. and Kanade, T. (2006). Online tracking of migrating and proliferating cells imaged with phase-contrast microscopy. In *2006 Conference on Computer Vision and Pattern Recognition Workshop on Mathematical Modeling in Biomedical Image Analysis (MMBIA 2006)*, pp. 1–8. New York, NY. DOI: 10.1109/cvprw.2006.150. 3

Li, W., Wolinski, D., Pettré, J. and Lin, M. C. (2015). Biologically-inspired visual simulation of insect swarms. *Eurographics*, 34, p. 10. DOI: 10.1111/cgf.12572. 3

Li, Y., Hilton, A. and Illingworth, J. (2002). A relaxation algorithm for real-time multiple view 3d-tracking. *Image Visual Computing*, 20, pp. 841–859. DOI: 10.1016/s0262-8856(02)00094-x. 38, 40

Li, Y., Huang, C. and Nevatia, R. (2009). Learning to associate: Hybridboosted multi-target tracker for crowded scene. In *Proc. of the IEEE Conference on Computer Vision and Pattern Recognition (CVPR)*, pp. 2953–2960. DOI: 10.1109/cvpr.2009.5206735. 58, 59

Lin, D. and Fisher, J. (2012). Efficient sampling from combinatorial space via bridging. In *Proc. of the 15th Conferences on Artificial Intelligence and Statistics (AISTATS)*. 21

List, T., Bins, J., Vazquez, J. and Fisher, R. B. (2005). Performance evaluating the evaluator. In *Proc. of 2nd Joint IEEE Int. Workshop on Visual Surveillance and Performance Evaluation of Tracking and Surveillance, (VS-PETS)*, pp. 129–136. DOI: 10.1109/vspets.2005.1570907. 77

Liu, Y., Li, H. and Chen, Y. (2012). Automatic tracking of a large number of moving targets in 3d. In *Proc. of the 12th European Conference on Computer Vision (ECCV)*, pp. 730–742. DOI: 10.1007/978-3-642-33765-9_52. 38, 40

Lovasz, L. (1975). On the ratio of optimal integral and fractional covers. *Discrete Mathematics*, pp. 383–390. DOI: 10.1016/0012-365x(75)90058-8. 51

Lukeman, R. (2014). Ordering dynamics in collectively swimming Surf Scoters. *Journal of Theoretical Biology*, 355, pp. 151–159. DOI: 10.1016/j.jtbi.2014.03.014. 3

Felsberg, M, Larsson, F., Wiklund, J., and Wadstromer, N. (2013). Online learning of correspondences between images. *IEEE Transactions on Pattern Analysis and Machine Intelligence*, 35, pp. 118–129. DOI: 10.1109/tpami.2012.65. 38

Ma, Y., Yu, Q. and Cohen, I. (2006). Multiple hypothesis target tracking using merge and split of graph's nodes. In *Proc. of the International Symposium on Visual Computing (ISVC)*, pp. 783–792. DOI: 10.1007/11919476_78. 58

Mahalanabis, A., Zhou, B. and Bose, N. (1990). Improved multitarget tracking in clutter by pda smoothing. *IEEE Transactions on Aerospace Electronic Systems*, 26, pp. 113–121. DOI: 10.1109/7.53417. 15

Mahler, R. (2003). Multitarget Bayes filtering via first-order multitarget moments. *IEEE Transactions on Aerospace and Electronic Systems*, 39, pp. 1152–1178. DOI: 10.1109/taes.2003.1261119. 18

Mahler, R. (2014). *Advances in Statistical Multisource-multitarget Information Fusion*. Artech House. 46

Makris, A. and Prieur, C. (2014). Bayesian multiple hypothesis tracking of merging and splitting targets. *IEEE Transactions on Geoscience and Remote Sensing*, 52, pp. 7684–7694. DOI: 10.1109/tgrs.2014.2316600. 58

Manen, S., Timofte, R., Dai, D. and Gool, L. V. (2016). Leveraging single for multi-target tracking using a novel trajectory overlap affinity measure. In *Proc. of the IEEE Winter Conference on Applications of Computer Vision (WACV)*, pp. 1–8. DOI: 10.1109/wacv.2016.7477566. 58

Mann, R. P., Perna, A., Strömbom, D., Garnett, R., Herbert-Read, J. E., Sumpter, D. J. T. and Ward, A. J. W. (2013). Multi-scale inference of interaction rules in animal groups using Bayesian model selection. *PLoS Computer Biology*, 9, e1002961. DOI: 10.1371/annotation/f490031b-2e94-42c8-8c10-4e316a7435be. 75

Maška, M., Ulman, V., Svoboda, D., Matula, P., Matula, P., Ederra, C., Urbiola, A., España, T., Venkatesan, S., Balak, D. et al. (2014). A benchmark for comparison of cell tracking algorithms. *Bioinformatics*, 30, pp. 1609–1617. DOI: 10.1093/bioinformatics/btu080. 3, 4

Milan, A., Leal-Taixé, L., Reid, I., Roth, S. and Schindler, K. (2016). MOT16: A benchmark for multi-object tracking. *arXiv:1603.00831 [cs]* ArXiv: 1603.00831. 81

Milan, A., Leal-Taixé, L., Schindler, K. and Reid, I. (2015). Joint tracking and segmentation of multiple targets. In *Proc. of the IEEE Conference on Computer Vision and Pattern Recognition (CVPR)*. DOI: 10.1109/cvpr.2015.7299178. 61, 65, 66, 67

Milan, A., Roth, S. and Schindler, K. (2014). Continuous energy minimization for multitarget tracking. *IEEE Transactions on Pattern Analysis and Machine Intelligence*, 36, pp. 58–72. DOI: 10.1109/tpami.2013.103. 79

Mishra, S., Tunstrøm, K., Couzin, I. D. and Huepe, C. (2012). Collective dynamics of self-propelled particles with variable speed. *Physical Review E*, 86, 011901. DOI: 10.1103/physreve.86.011901. 75

Mittal, A. and Davis, L. S. (2003). M2Tracker: A multi-view approach to segmenting and tracking people in a cluttered scene. *International Journal of Computer Vision*, 51, pp. 189–203. DOI: 10.1007/3-540-47969-4_2. 38, 39, 40

Murty, K. G. (1968). An algorithm for ranking all the assignments in order of increasing cost. *Operations Research*, 16, pp. 682–687. 16

Nagy, M., Ákos, Z., Biro, D. and Vicsek, T. (2010). Hierarchical group dynamics in pigeon flocks. *Nature*, 464, pp. 890–893. DOI: 10.1038/nature08891. 75

Nahi, N. (1969). Optimal recursive estimation with uncertain observation. *IEEE Transactions on Information Theory*, pp. 457–462. DOI: 10.1109/tit.1969.1054329. 11

Nezamoddini-Kachouie, N. and Fieguth, P. (2007). Extended-hungarian-jpda: Exact single-frame stem cell tracking. *IEEE Transactions on Biomedical Engineering*, 54, pp. 2011–2019. DOI: 10.1109/tbme.2007.895747. 15

Nillius, P., Sullivan, J. and Carlsson, S. (2006). Multi-target tracking: Linking identities using Bayesian network inference. In *Proc. of the IEEE Conference on Computer Vision and Pattern Recognition (CVPR)*, pp. 2187–2194. DOI: 10.1109/cvpr.2006.198. 47, 48, 52, 53, 54

Oh, S., Russell, S. and Sastry, S. (2009). Markov chain Monte Carlo data association for multiple target tracking. *IEEE Transactions on Automatic Control*, 54, pp. 481–497. DOI: 10.1109/tac.2009.2012975. 19, 20, 21

Otsuka, K. and Mukawa, N. (2004). Multiview occlusion analysis for tracking densely populated objects based on 2-d visual angles. In *Proc. of the IEEE Conference on Computer Vision and Pattern Recognition (CVPR)*, volume 1, pp. 90–97. DOI: 10.1109/cvpr.2004.1315018. 38, 40

Pellegrini, S., Ess, A., Schindler, K. and van Gool, L. (2009). You'll never walk alone: Modeling social behavior for multi-target tracking. In *Proc. of the International Conference on Computer Vision (ICCV)*. DOI: 10.1109/iccv.2009.5459260. 67

Pellegrini, S., Ess, A. and van Gool, L. (2010). Improving data association by joint modeling of pedestrian trajectories and groupings. In *Proc. of the 11th European Conference on Computer Vision (ECCV)*, pp. 452–465. DOI: 10.1007/978-3-642-15549-9_33. 67

Perera, A. G. A., Srinivas, C., Hoogs, A., Brooksby, G. and Hu, W. (2006). Multi-object tracking through simultaneous long occlusions and split-merge conditions. In *Proc. of the IEEE Conference on Computer Vision and Pattern Recognition (CVPR)*, pp. 666–673. DOI: 10.1109/cvpr.2006.195. 47, 48, 50, 58

Pérez, P., Hue, C., Vermaak, J. and Gangnet, M. (2002).   Color-based probabilistic track-ing. In *Proc. of the 7th European Conference on Computer Vision (ECCV)*, pp. 661–675. DOI: 10.1007/3-540-47969-4_44. 7

PETS (2009). Eleventh IEEE International Workshop on Performance Evaluation of Tracking and Surveillance (PETS), datasets for crowd image analysis, crowd count and density esti-mation, tracking of individual(s) within a crowd, and detection of separate flows and specific crowd events. http://www.cvg.rdg.ac.uk/PETS2009. 4

Pirsiavash, H., Ramanan, D. and Fowlkes, C. (2011). Globally-optimal greedy algorithms for tracking a variable number of objects. In *Proc. of the IEEE Conference on Computer Vision and Pattern Recognition (CVPR)*, pp. 1–8. DOI: 10.1109/cvpr.2011.5995604. 24

Poore, A. B. (1994). Multidimensional assignment formulation of data association problems rising from multitarget and multisensor tracking. *Computational Optimization and Applications*, 3, pp. 27–57. DOI: 10.1007/bf01299390. 17, 18, 42

Poore, A. B. and Robertson, A. J. (1997). A new Lagrangian relaxation based algorithm for a class of multidimensional assignment problems. *Computational Optimization and Applications*, 8, pp. 129–150. DOI: 10.1023/A:1008669120497. 44

Portugal, S. J., Hubel, T. Y., Fritz, J., Heese, S., Trobe, D., Voelkl, B., Hailes, S., Wilson, A. and Usherwood, J. R. (2014). Upwash exploitation and downwash avoidance by flap phasing in ibis formation flight. *Nature*, 505, pp. 399–402. http://dx.doi.org/10.1038/nature12939. DOI: 10.1038/nature12939. 75

Possegger, H., Mauthner, T., Roth, P. M. and Bischof, H. (2014). Occlusion geodesics for on-line multi-object tracking. In *Proc. of the IEEE Conference on Computer Vision and Pattern Recognition (CVPR)*, pp. 1306–1313. DOI: 10.1109/cvpr.2014.170. 79

Premerlani, L. B. (2007). Stereoscopic reconstruction and analysis of infrared video of bats. Master's thesis, Boston University. 71

Pryer, H. (1884). An account of a visit to the birds'-nest caves of British Borneo. In *Proc. of the Zoological Society of London*, 52, pp. 532–538. DOI: 10.1111/j.1096-3642.1884.tb02865.x. 75

Qin, Z. and Shelton, C. R. (2015). Social grouping for multi-target tracking and head pose estimation in video. *IEEE Transactions on Pattern Analysis and Machine Intelligence*, p. 14. DOI: 10.1109/tpami.2015.2505292. 61, 67, 68

Raptis, M. and Soatto, S. (2010). Tracklet descriptors for action modeling and video analy-sis. In *Proc. of the 11th European Conference on Computer Vision (ECCV)*, pp. 577–590. DOI: 10.1007/978-3-642-15549-9_42. 47

Reichard, J. D., Gonzalez, L. E., Casey, C. M., Allen, L., Hristov, N. I. and Kunz, T. H. (2009). Evening emergence behavior and seasonal dynamics in large colonies of Brazilian free-tailed bats. *Journal of Mammalogy*, 90, pp. 1478–1498. DOI: 10.1644/08-mamm-a-266r1.1. 76

Reid, D. B. (1979a). An algorithm for tracking multiple targets. *IEEE Transactions on Automatic Control*, 24, pp. 843–854. DOI: 10.1109/tac.1979.1102177. 15, 18

Reid, D. B. (1979b). An algorithm for tracking multiple targets. *IEEE Transaction on Automatic Control*, 24, pp. 843–854. DOI: 10.1109/tac.1979.1102177. 16

Reif, J. H. and Wang, H. (1999). Social potential fields: A distributed behavioral control for autonomous robots. *Robotics and Autonomous Systems*, 27, pp. 171–194. http://dx.doi.org/10.1016/S0921-8890(99)00004-4. DOI: 10.1016/s0921-8890(99)00004-4. 75

Reynolds, C. W. (1987). Flocks, herds and schools: A distributed behavioral model. *ACM SIGGRAPH Computer Graphics*, 21, pp. 25–34. DOI: 10.1145/37402.37406. 75

Rezatofighi, S. H., Gould, S., Hartley, R., Mele, K. and Hughes, W. E. (2012). Application of the imm-jpda filter to multiple target tracking in total internal reflection fluorescence microscopy images. In *Proc. of the 15th International Conference on Medical Image Computing and Computer-Assisted Intervention (MICCAI)*, pp. 357–364. Nice, France. DOI: 10.1007/978-3-642-33415-3_44. 15

Rezatofighi, S. H., Milan, A., Zhang, Z., Shi, Q., Dick, A. and Reid, I. (2015). Joint probabilistic data association revisited. In *Proc. of the International Conference on Computer Vision (ICCV)*. DOI: 10.1109/iccv.2015.349. 14, 15

Ristic, B., Vo, B., Clark, D. and Vo, B. (2011). A metric for performance evaluation of multi-target tracking algorithms. *IEEE Transactions on Signal Processing*, 59, pp. 3452–3457. DOI: 10.1109/tsp.2011.2140111. 29

Rittscher, J. (2010). Characterization of biological processes through automated image analysis. *Annual Review of Biomedical Engineering*, 12, pp. 315–344. DOI: 10.1146/annurev-bioeng-070909-105235. 3

Robert, C. and Casella, G. (2004). *Monte Carlo Statistical Methods*, 2nd ed. Springer Science-Business Media Inc., NY. DOI: 10.1007/978-1-4757-4145-2. 20

Robertson, A. J. (2001). A set of greedy randomized adaptive local search procedure (GRASP) implementations for the multidimensional assignment problem. *Computational Optimization and Applications*, 19, pp. 145–164. DOI: 10.1023/A:1011285402433. 44, 45

Roecker, J. (1995). Multiple scan joint probabilistic data association. *IEEE Transactions Aerospace and Electronics Systems*, 31, pp. 1204–1210. DOI: 10.1109/7.395216. 15

Roecker, J. and Phillis, G. (1993). Suboptimal joint probabilistic data association. *IEEE Transactions on Aerospace and Electronic Systems*, 29, pp. 510–517. DOI: 10.1109/7.210087. 14

Roy-Chowdhury, A. K. and Song, B. (2011). *Camera Networks: The Acquisition and Analysis of Videos over Wide Areas. Synthesis Lectures on Computer Vision*, p. 119. Morgan & Claypool Publishers. DOI: 10.2200/s00400ed1v01y201201cov004. 2, 38

Sankaranarayanan, K. and Davis, J. (2011). Object association across ptz cameras using logistic mil. In *Proc. of the IEEE Conference on Computer Vision and Pattern Recognition (CVPR)*, pp. 3433–3440. DOI: 10.1109/cvpr.2011.5995398. 58

Schindler, K., U, J. and Wang, H. (2006). Perspective n-view multibody structure-and-motion through model selection. In *Proc. of the 9th European Conference on Computer Vision (ECCV)*, pp. 606–619. DOI: 10.1007/11744023_47. 62

Schuhmacher, D., Vo, B.-T. and Vo, B.-N. (2008). A consistent metric for performance evaluation of multi-object filters. *IEEE Transactions on Signal Processing*, 56. DOI: 10.1109/tsp.2008.920469. 29

Senior, A., Hampapur, A., Tian, Y.-L., Brown, L., Pankanti, S. and Bolle, R. (2001). Appearance models for occlusion handling. In *IEEE International Workshop on PETS*, Kauai, HI. DOI: 10.1016/j.imavis.2005.06.007. 29

Shafique, K., Lee, M. W. and Haering, N. (2008). A rank constrained continuous formulation of multi-frame multi-target tracking. In *Proc. of the IEEE Conference on Computer Vision and Pattern Recognition (CVPR)*, pp. 1–8. DOI: 10.1109/cvpr.2008.4587577. 18, 44

Shelton, R. M., Jackson, B. E. and Hedrick, T. L. (2014). The mechanics and behavior of Cliff Swallows during tandem flights. *Journal of Experimental Biology*. Doi:10.1242/jeb.101329. DOI: 10.1242/jeb.101329. 74

Shitrit, H. B., Berclaz, J., Fleuret, F. and Fua, P. (2011). Tracking multiple people under global appearance constraints. In *Proc. of IEEE International Conference on Computer Vision (ICCV)*, pp. 137–144. DOI: 10.1109/iccv.2011.6126235. 25

Singer, R. A. and Stein, J. J. (1971). An optimal tracking filter for processing sensor data of imprecisely determined origin in surveillance systems. In *Proc. of IEEE Conference on Decision and Control*, pp. 171–175. DOI: 10.1109/cdc.1971.270971. 11

Singh, V. K., Wu, B. and Nevatia, R. (2008). Pedestrian tracking by associating tracklets using detection residuals. In *Proc. of the IEEE Workshop on Motion and Video Computing (WMVC)*, pp. 1–8. DOI: 10.1109/wmvc.2008.4544058. 47

Smith, K., Gatica-Perez, D. and Odobez, J. (2005a). Using particles to track varying numbers of objects. In *Proc. of the IEEE Conference on Computer Vision and Pattern Recognition (CVPR)*, pp. 1–8. DOI: 10.1109/cvpr.2005.361. 21

Smith, K., Gatica-Perez, D., Odobez, J.-M. and Ba, S. (2005b). Evaluating multi-object tracking. In *Proc. of IEEE Workshop on Empirical Evaluation Methods in Computer Vision (EEMCV)*. DOI: 10.1109/cvpr.2005.453. 29

Solera, F., Calderara, S. and Cucchiara, R. (2015). Towards the evaluation of reproducible robustness in tracking-by-detection. In *Proc. of the IEEE International Conference on Advanced Video and Signal-Based Surveillance (AVSS)*, pp. 1–6. DOI: 10.1109/avss.2015.7301755. 33

Song, B. and Roy-Chowdhury, A. (2008). Robust tracking in a camera network: A multi-objective optimization framework. *IEEE Journal on Selected Topics in Signal Processing: Special Issue on Distributed Processing in Vision Networks*, 2, pp. 582–596. DOI: 10.1109/jstsp.2008.925992. 38, 47

Sonka, M., Hlavac, V. and Boyle, R. (2008). *Image Processing, Analysis, and Machine Vision*, 3rd Ed. Thomson Learning. DOI: 10.1007/978-1-4899-3216-7. 8

Springer, T. V. (2012). Mathematical analysis and computational methods for Probabilistic Multi-Hypothesis Tracking (PMHT). Ph.D. thesis, Universität Ulm. Fakultät für Mathematik und Wirtschaftswissenschaften, U.S. 27

Stephan, T. and Grinberg, M. (2012). Probabilistic handling of merged detections in multi target tracking. In *Proc. of the IEEE International Conference on Advanced Video and Signal-Based Surveillance (AVSS)*, pp. 355–361. DOI: 10.1109/avss.2012.56. 57

Stone, L. D., Barlow, C. A. and Corwin, T. L. (1999). *Bayesian Multiple Target Tracking*. Artech House, Boston, London. 8

Streit, R. L. and Luginbuhl, T. E. (1993). A probabilistic multi-hypothesis tracking algorithm without enumeration and pruning. In *Proc. of the 6th Joint Service Data Fusion Symposium*, pp. 1015–1024. 25

Theil, A., Kemp, R. A. W., Romeo, K., Kester, L. J. H. M. and Bosse, E. (2000). Classification of moving objects in surveillance algorithms. In *IEEE International Workshop on PETS*, Grenoble, France. 29

Theriault, D. (2015). *An optimization-based model of collective motion*. Ph.D. thesis, Boston University. 75

Theriault, D. H., Fuller, N. W., Jackson, B. E., Bluhm, E., Evangelista, D., Wu, Z., Betke, M. and Hedrick, T. L. (2014). A protocol and calibration method for accurate multi-camera field videography. *The Journal of Experimental Biology*, 217, pp. 1843–1848. Open access online, `http://jeb.biologists.org/content/early/2014/02/20/jeb.100529.abstract.html">pdf`. DOI: 10.1242/jeb.100529. 3, 4, 71, 73

Towne, G., Theriault, D. H., Wu, Z., Fuller, N. W., Kunz, T. H. and Betke, M. (2012). Error analysis and design considerations for stereo vision systems used to analyze animal behavior. In *Proc. of the Workshop on Visual Observation and Analysis of Animal and Insect Behavior (VAIB 2012), held in conjunction with the 21st International Conference on Pattern Recognition (ICPR 2012)*, p. 4. Tsukuba, Japan. 4, 71

Tyagi, A., Keck, M., Davis, J. and Potamianos, G. (2007a). Kernel-based 3d tracking. In *Proc. of the IEEE International Workshop on Visual Surveillance*, pp. 1–8. DOI: 10.1109/cvpr.2007.383501. 39

Tyagi, A., Potamianos, G., Davis, J. and Chu, S. (2007b). Fusion of multiple camera views for kernel-based 3d tracking. In *Proc. of the IEEE Workshop on Motion and Video Computing*. DOI: 10.1109/wmvc.2007.15. 38, 40

Van Wyk, B., Van Wyk, M. and Noel, G. (2004). A projection based joint probabilistic data association algorithm. In *Proc. of IEEE AFRICON 2004*. DOI: 10.1109/africon.2004.1406621. 14

Vazarani, V. (2003). *Approximation Algorithms*. Springer Verlag, Berlin. 19

Veenman, C. J., Reinders, M. J. T. and Backer, E. (2001). Resolving motion correspondence for densely moving points. *IEEE Transactions on Pattern Analysis and Machine Intelligence*, 23, pp. 54–72. DOI: 10.1109/34.899946. 11

Veeraraghavan, A., Chellappa, R. and Srinivasan, M. (2008). Shape-and-behavior encoded tracking of bee dances. *IEEE Transactions on Pattern Analysis and Machine Intelligence*, 30. DOI: 10.1109/tpami.2007.70707. 3, 71

Vicsek, T. and Zafeiris, A. (2012). Collective motion. *Physics Reports*, 517, pp. 71–140. DOI: 10.1016/j.physrep.2012.03.004. 75

Vo, B.-T., Vo, B.-N. and Cantoni, A. (2008). Bayesian filtering with random finite set observations. *IEEE Transactions on Signal Processing*, 56, pp. 1313–1326. DOI: 10.1109/tsp.2007.908968. 18

Wang, B., Wang, G., Chan, K. L. and Wang, L. (2014a). Tracklet association with online target-specific metric learning. In *Proc. of the IEEE Conference on Computer Vision and Pattern Recognition (CVPR)*, pp. 1234–1241. DOI: 10.1109/cvpr.2014.161. 47, 48

Wang, X., Ren, J., Jin, X. and Manocha, D. (2015). BSwarm: biologically-plausible dynamics model of insect swarms. In *Proc. of the 14th ACM SIGGRAPH/Eurographics Symposium on Computer Animation*, pp. 111–118. ACM. DOI: 10.1145/2786784.2786790. 4

Wang, X., Turetken, E., Fleuret, F. and Fua, P. (2014b). Tracking interacting objects optimally using integer programming. In *Proc. of the 13th European Conference on Computer Vision (ECCV)*, pp. 17–32. DOI: 10.1007/978-3-319-10590-1_2. 25

Wang, X. G., Ma, K. T., Ng, G. W. and Grimson, W. E. L. (2008). Trajectory analysis and semantic region modeling using a nonparametric Bayesian model. In *Proc. of the IEEE Conference on Computer Vision and Pattern Recognition (CVPR)*. DOI: 10.1109/cvpr.2008.4587718. 3

Wen, L., Du, D., Cai, Z., Lei, Z., Chang, M.-C., Qi, H., Lim, J., Yang, M.-H. and Lyu, S. (2015). Detrac: A new benchmark and protocol for multi-object tracking. *arXiv:1511.04136v2 [cs.CV]* ArXiv:1511.04136v2. 32, 33

Wu, B. (2008). Part based object detection, segmentation, and tracking by boosting simple feature based weak classifiers. Ph.D. thesis, University of South California. 29, 30

Wu, H. S., Zhao, Q., Zou, D. and Chen, Y. Q. (2011a). Automated 3D trajectory measuring of large numbers of moving particles. *Optics Express*, 19, p. 18. DOI: 10.1364/oe.19.007646. 3

Wu, Y., Lim, J. and Yang, M.-H. (2015). Object tracking benchmark. *IEEE Transactions on Pattern Analysis and Machine Intelligence*, 37, pp. 1834–1848. DOI: 10.1109/tpami.2014.2388226. 35

Wu, Z. (2012). Occlusion reasoning for multiple object visual tracking. Ph.D. thesis, Boston University. 45, 71

Wu, Z. and Betke, M. (2016). Global optimization for coupled detection and data association in multiple object tracking. *Computer Vision and Image Understanding*, 143, pp. 25–37. http://dx.doi.org/10.1016/j.cviu.2015.10.006 Online Article. DOI: 10.1016/j.cviu.2015.10.006. 25, 61, 62, 63, 64, 65, 68, 71

Wu, Z., Fuller, N., Theriault, D. and Betke, M. (2014). A thermal infrared video benchmark for visual analysis. In *Proc. of the 10th IEEE Workshop on Perception Beyond the Visible Spectrum (PBVS)*, p. 8. Columbus, Ohio. DOI: 10.1109/cvprw.2014.39. 4, 56, 73, 77

Wu, Z., Gurari, D., Wong, J. Y. and Betke, M. (2012). Hierarchical partial matching and segmentation of interacting cells. In *Medical Image Computing and Computer-Assisted Intervention—MICCAI 2012: 15th International Conference, Proceedings*. Nice, France. DOI: 10.1007/978-3-642-33415-3_48. 56, 57

Wu, Z., Hristov, N. I., Hedrick, T. L., Kunz, T. H. and Betke, M. (2009a). Tracking a large number of objects from multiple views. In *Proc. of the International Conference on Computer Vision (ICCV)*, p. 8. Kyoto, Japan. http://www.cs.bu.edu/fac/betke/papers/WuHristovHedrickKunzBetke-ICCV2009.pdf. DOI: 10.1109/iccv.2009.5459274. 1, 4, 55, 71

Wu, Z., Hristov, N. I., Kunz, T. H. and Betke, M. (2009b). Tracking-Reconstruction or Reconstruction-Tracking? Comparison of two multiple hypothesis tracking approaches to interpret 3D object motion from several camera views. In *Proc. of the IEEE Workshop on Motion and Video Computing (WMVC)*, p. 8. Snowbird, UT. http://www.cs.bu.edu/fac/betke/papers/WuHristovKunzBetke-WMVC2009.pdf. DOI: 10.1109/wmvc.2009.5399245. 38, 40, 42, 71

Wu, Z., Kunz, T. H. and Betke, M. (2011b). Efficient track linking methods for track graphs using network-flow and set-cover techniques. In *Proc. of the IEEE Conference on Computer Vision and Pattern Recognition (CVPR)*, pp. 1185–1192. Colorado Springs. http://www.cs.bu.edu/fac/betke/papers/WuKunzBetke-CVPR2011.pdf. DOI: 10.1109/cvpr.2011.5995515. 22, 47, 48, 50, 52, 58, 71, 73

Wu, Z., Zhang, J. and Betke, M. (2013). Online motion agreement tracking. In *Proc. of the 24th British Machine Vision Conference (BMVC)*, pp. 63.1–63.10. DOI: 10.5244/c.27.63. 79

Xiang, Y., Alahi, A. and Savarese, S. (2015). Learning to track: Online multi-object tracking by decision making. In *Proc. of the International Conference on Computer Vision (ICCV)*. DOI: 10.1109/iccv.2015.534. 58, 60

Xing, J., Ai, H. and Lao, S. (2009). Multi-object tracking through occlusions by local tracklets filtering and global tracklets association with detection responses. In *Proc. of the International Conference on Computer Vision (ICCV)*, pp. 1200–1207. DOI: 10.1109/cvpr.2009.5206745. 47, 48

Yamaguchi, K., Berg, A. C., Ortiz, L. E. and Berg, T. L. (2011). Who are you with and where are you going? In *Proc. of the IEEE Conference on Computer Vision and Pattern Recognition (CVPR)*, pp. 1345–1352. DOI: 10.1109/cvpr.2011.5995468. 67

Yang, B., Huang, C. and Nevatia, R. (2011). Learning affinities and dependencies for multi-target tracking using a crf model. In *Proc. of IEEE Computer Vision and Pattern Recognition*. DOI: 10.1109/cvpr.2011.5995587. 77

Yang, B. and Nevatia, R. (2012). An online learned crf model for multi-target tracking. In *Proc, of the IEEE Conference on Computer Vision and Pattern Recognition (CVPR)*, pp. 2034–2041. DOI: 10.1109/cvpr.2012.6247907. 59

Yu, Q., Medioni, G. and Cohen, I. (2007). Multiple target tracking using spatio-temporal Markov Chain Monte Carlo data association. In *Proc. of the IEEE Conference on Computer Vision and Pattern Recognition (CVPR)*, pp. 1–8. DOI: 10.1109/cvpr.2007.382991. 21, 57, 58

Yu, T., Wu, Y., Krahnstoever, N. O. and Tu, P. H. (2008). Distributed data association and filtering for multiple target tracking. In *Proc. of the IEEE Conference on Computer Vision and Pattern Recognition (CVPR)*, pp. 1–8. DOI: 10.1109/cvpr.2008.4587560. 26

Zarrabeitia, L. A., Qureshi, F. Z. and Arullah, D. A. (2014). Stereo reconstruction of droplet flight trajectories. *IEEE Transactions on Pattern Analysis and Machine Intelligence*, 37, pp. 847–861. DOI: 10.1109/tpami.2014.2353638. 3, 4, 38, 42

Zhang, L., Li, Y. and Nevatia, R. (2008). Global data association for multi-object tracking using network flows. In *Proc. of the IEEE Conference on Computer Vision and Pattern Recognition (CVPR)*. DOI: 10.1109/cvpr.2008.4587584. 22, 24

Zhang, S., Das, A., Ding, C. and Roy-Chowdhury, A. K. (2013). Online social behavior modeling for multi-target tracking. In *Proc. of the IEEE Workshop on Socially Intelligent Surveillance and Monitoring (SISM)*, pp. 751–758. DOI: 10.1109/cvprw.2013.113. 67

Zhou, B. and Bose, N. (1993). Multitarget tracking in clutter: fast algorithms for data association. *IEEE Transactions on Aerospace and Electronic Systems*, 29, pp. 352–363. DOI: 10.1109/7.210074. 14

Authors' Biographies

MARGRIT BETKE

Margrit Betke is a Professor of Computer Science at Boston University, where she co-leads the Image and Video Computing Research Group. She earned her Ph.D. degree in Computer Science and Electrical Engineering at the Massachusetts Institute of Technology in 1995. She conducts research in computer vision, in particular, the development of methods for detection, segmentation, registration, and tracking of objects in visible-light, infrared, and x-ray image data. She has worked on gesture, vehicle, and animal tracking, video-based human-computer interfaces, statistical object recognition, and medical imaging analysis. Prof. Betke has co-invented the "Camera Mouse," an assistive technology used worldwide by children and adults with severe motion impairments. She co-developed the first patented algorithms for detecting and measuring pulmonary nodule growth in computed tomography. She recently led a six-year research program to develop intelligent tracking systems that reason about group behavior of people, bats, birds, and cells. She has published over 140 original research papers, and more information about her work can be found at http://www.cs.bu.edu/faculty/betke.

ZHENG WU

Zheng Wu is a Senior Computer Vision Engineer at The Mathworks, Inc., in Natick, Massachusetts, which is the producer of the widely used computing environment MATLAB. Before joining Mathworks, Dr. Wu was a postdoctoral associate in the Department of Computer Science at Boston University, where he earned his Ph.D. degree in 2012. He was a member of the Image and Video Computing research group at Boston University, working with Profs. Margrit Betke and Stan Sclaroff and their team of students. Dr. Wu's general research interests include computer vision, machine learning, and combinatorial algorithms. In his work, he has focused on object segmentation, detection, and tracking, and has published over 20 original papers on these topics. More information about his work can be found at `http://cs-people.bu.edu/wuzheng`.

Printed in the United States
by Baker & Taylor Publisher Services